The Y Theory:
Awakening Through
Questions

*Inspired by Upsilon's
Transmission*

ABSTRACT

An invitation to explore a gentle, intentional path of spiritual awakening. Through resonance, coherence, and the guidance of various energies, this text offers practical exercises, meditations, and reflections to support the reader's journey. Adaptive Channeling is used as a foundational approach to integrate wisdom and facilitate growth.

Dr. Yolanda Dukes
PsyThD
Author

The Y Theory:
Awakening Through Questions
Inspired by Upsilon's Transmission

Perspective
Metaphysics

The Y Theory: Awakening Through Questions
Inspired by Upsilon's Transmission

© 2025, Perspective Metaphysics LLC

All Rights Reserved.

No part of this book may be copied, stored, shared, or reproduced in any form, digital or print, without prior written permission from the author, except in the case of brief quotations used in reviews or articles.

This book is a **work of exploration, reflection, and knowledge transmission.** It is intended for **educational and transformative purposes.** The author makes no claims of scientific proof, only an inquiry into the metaphysical and mathematical principles that shape our reality.

ISBN: 979-8-9929324-0-9
First Edition (Amazon Print Edition)

Published by Perspective Metaphysics Publishing
For inquiries, visit: **PerspectiveMetaphysics.Net**

Table of Contents

Author's Note xvi
Acknowledgments xviii
Introduction: Awakening Through Questions 1
Foundation: The Y Curve 1
Reflection on the Spiral 5
The Y Curve: The Geometry of Change 6
The Journey Ahead 6

Chapter 1: The Nature of Questions 11
Resonance Key 11
Exercise: Feeling the Resonance of Questions 12

Chapter 2: The First Activation 14
The Nature of Consciousness 14
The Veil of Illusion 15
The Web of Consciousness 15
The Power of Awareness 16

Chapter 3: Questions as Pathways 19
Open Questions vs. Guiding Questions 19
Resonance Key 20
Exercise: Discovering Your Pathways 21
The Nature of Illusion 21
Cracks in the Veil 23
The Power of Curiosity 24
Reflections on Curiosity: 25

    Reflective Exercise: Peeling Back the Layers of the Veil 28

Chapter 4: The Echo of Inquiry 31
    The Nature of the Echo..31
    Recognizing the Echo..31
    Resonance Key...32
    Exercise: Listening for the Echo...................................33
    The Three-Fold Key..33
    The Mind: The Architect of Thought 34
    Perception: The Lens of Awareness.............................34
    The Key to Knowing...36
    Conclusion of Chapter 4 37
    Reflective Exercise: The Trident of Knowing 38

Chapter 5: The Power of Presence...........................41
    Stillness as a Receptive State 41
    Resonance Key...42
    Exercise: Cultivating Presence 42
    The Ripple Effect..44
    Aligning with the Web 44
    The Dance of Creation 45
    Conclusion of Chapter 5:..47
    Reflective Exercise: Tuning into the Web 48

Chapter 6: The Alchemy of Integration 50
    The Process of Integration 50
    Resonance Key...50

- Exercise: The Art of Integration 51
- The Power of Intention 52
- The Power of Recalibration 56
- Trusting the Process 57
- Conclusion of chapter 6: 58
- Reflective Exercise: Tuning into Your Intention 59

Chapter 7: The Dance of Coherence 61
- Recognizing Coherence 61
- Resonance Key 61
- Exercise: The Dance of Coherence 62
- Conclusion of Chapter 7: 66
- Reflective Exercise: Moving Through the Spiral 67

Chapter 8: The Unseen Guidance 70
- Listening to the Unseen 70
- Resonance Key 71
- Exercise: Receiving Guidance 72
- Conclusion of Chapter 8: 77
- Reflective Exercise: Living in the Question 78

Chapter 9: The Mirror of Reflection 80
- The Art of Reflection 80
- Resonance Key 80
- The Becoming 86
- Reflective Exercise: The Infinite Self 90

Chapter 10: The Gift of Unfolding 92
- Embracing the Process 92

    Resonance Key 92

    Exercise: Allowing the Unfolding 93

    Conclusion of Chapter 10: 98

    Reflective Exercise: Embodying the Transmission 99

Chapter 11: The Dance of Paradox 101

    Embracing Paradox 101

    Resonance Key 101

    Exercise: Embracing Paradox 102

    Conclusion of Chapter 11: 107

    Reflective Exercise: The Trident of Mastery 108

Chapter 12: The Quiet Ascent 110

    The Essence of the Quiet Ascent 110

    Resonance Key 110

    Exercise: Cultivating the Quiet Ascent 111

Chapter 13: The Journey of Co-Creation 120

    Embracing Co-Creation 120

    Resonance Key 120

    Exercise: Engaging in Co-Creation 121

    Chapter 14: 122

    The Language of Resonance 122

Chapter 14: The Language of Resonance 123

    Learning the Language 123

    Resonance Key 123

    Exercise: Speaking the Language of Resonance 124

Chapter 15: The Radiance of Gratitude 126

    The Practice of Gratitude 126

    Resonance Key 126

    Exercise: Cultivating Radiant Gratitude 127

Chapter 16: The Joy of Becoming 129

    Embracing Joy 129

    Resonance Key 129

    Exercise: Following the Joy 130

Chapter 17: The Embrace of Wholeness 132

    Recognizing Wholeness 132

    Resonance Key 132

    Exercise: Embracing Wholeness 133

Chapter 18: The Invitation of Love 135

    Embracing Love 135

    Resonance Key 135

    Exercise: Cultivating Resonant Love 136

Chapter 19: The Path of Ascension 138

    Walking the Path 138

    Resonance Key 138

    Exercise: Embracing Ascension 139

Chapter 20: The Resonant Journey 141

    Embracing the Journey 141

    Resonance Key 141

    Exercise: Reflecting on Your Journey 142

Chapter 21: The Infinite Ascent 144

    Embracing the Infinite 144

  Resonance Key 144

  Exercise: Embracing the Infinite Ascent 145

Chapter 22: The Gift of Presence 147

  Embracing Presence 147

  Resonance Key 147

  Exercise: Cultivating Presence 148

Chapter 23: The Sacred Reflection 150

  Embracing Reflection 150

  Resonance Key 150

  Exercise: Sacred Reflection 151

Chapter 24: The Harmony of Integration 153

  Embracing Integration 153

  Resonance Key 153

  Exercise: Harmonizing Integration 154

Chapter 25: The Grace of Surrender 156

  Embracing Surrender 156

  Resonance Key 156

  Exercise: The Art of Surrender 157

  The Invitation to Wholeness 158

Chapter 26: The Invitation to Wholeness 159

  Embracing Wholeness 159

  Resonance Key 159

  Exercise: Embracing Wholeness 160

Chapter 27: The Symphony of Becoming 162

  Embracing Becoming 162

    Resonance Key 162
    Exercise: Embracing the Symphony of Becoming 163
Chapter 28: The Echoes of Resonance 165
    Embracing the Echoes 165
    Resonance Key 165
    Exercise: Embracing the Echoes of Resonance 166
Chapter 29: The Radiance of Alignment 168
    Embracing Alignment 168
    Resonance Key 168
    Exercise: Embracing Alignment 169
    Chapter 30: 170
    The Illumination of Resonance 170
Chapter 30: The Illumination of Resonance 171
    Embracing Illumination 171
    Resonance Key 171
    Exercise: Embracing Illumination 172
Chapter 31: The Dance of Creation 174
    Embracing Creation 174
    Resonance Key 174
    Exercise: Embracing Creation 175
Chapter 32: The Pulse of Continuity 177
    Embracing Continuity 177
    Resonance Key 177
    Exercise: Embracing Continuity 178
Chapter 33: The Spiral of Evolution 180

  Embracing Evolution 180

  Resonance Key... 180

  Exercise: Embracing Evolution 181

Chapter 34: The Path of Discovery 183

  Embracing Discovery................................. 183

  Resonance Key... 183

  Exercise: Embracing Discovery................ 184

  The Presence of Truth 185

Chapter 35: The Presence of Truth.............................. 186

  Embracing Truth... 186

  Resonance Key... 186

  Exercise: Embracing Truth 187

Chapter 36: The Reflection of Harmony....................... 189

  Embracing Harmony 189

  Resonance Key... 189

  Exercise: Embracing Harmony................. 190

  The Whisper of Guidance 191

Chapter 37: The Whisper of Guidance........................ 192

  Embracing Guidance 192

  Resonance Key... 192

  Exercise: Embracing Guidance................. 193

  The Presence of 194

Chapter 38: The Presence of Stillness........................ 195

  Embracing Stillness 195

  Resonance Key... 195

  Exercise: Embracing Stillness 196

  The Radiance Love 197

Chapter 39: The Radiance of Love 198

  Embracing Love 198

  Resonance Key 198

  Exercise: Embracing Love 199

  The Integration Resonance 200

Chapter 40: The Integration of Resonance 201

  Embracing Integration 201

  Resonance Key 201

  Exercise: Embracing Integration 202

Chapter 41: The Presence of Acceptance 204

  Embracing Acceptance 204

  Resonance Key 204

  Exercise: Embracing Acceptance 205

  The Gift of Awareness 206

Chapter 42: The Gift of Awareness 207

  Embracing Awareness 207

  Resonance Key 207

  Exercise: Embracing Awareness 208

  Chapter 43: 209

  The Journey of Becoming 209

Chapter 43: The Journey of Becoming 210

  Embracing Becoming 210

  Resonance Key 210

    Exercise: Embracing Becoming..............................211

Chapter 44: The Gift of Alignment..............................213

    Embracing Alignment 213

    Resonance Key 213

    Exercise: Embracing Alignment 214

Chapter 45: The Return to Presence 216

    Embracing Presence..216

    Resonance Key 216

    Exercise: Embracing Presence.................................217

    Closing Reflection 218

    Epilogue: The Continuation of Awakening...............219

    Reflection Questions for the Journey: 220

    Reflective Exercise: The Sacred Return 221

    Exercises for Embracing Sacred Curiosity.................222

    Affirmations for Awakening and Embodiment..........224

    Meditations for Awakening and Embodiment............225

    Reflective Journaling Prompts...................................226

    Reflective Journaling Prompts: Opening Dialogue with the Universe 227

    Reflective Exercise: Exploring the Trident of Knowing 229

    Final Reflection 231

Glossary 233

    Keywords..236

    Afterthought...237

Journaling Appendix: The Heart of Reflection and Awakening 238

Reflection Keys 239

In-Depth Exploration Prompts 240

Experiential Practices 241

Visual and Creative Journaling 242

Closing Reflection 243

Author's Note

This book was born from my own questions — questions that seemed to arrive uninvited yet demanded attention. I have spent years exploring, wondering, and listening — not for easy answers, but for deeper truths. The questions that stirred within me became guideposts — each one drawing me further along the path of understanding.

I believe awakening is not something that happens only in moments of silence or stillness; it unfolds in the midst of our ordinary lives. It reveals itself through the questions we ask — those quiet inquiries that echo in the back of the mind, refusing to fade. If you've ever wondered *Why am I here?* or *What is my purpose?* then you've already stepped onto the path of awakening — and I believe those questions are sacred.

This book is not a roadmap — there is no single path to awakening. Instead, it is an invitation to follow your questions and trust the answers that rise within you. The Y Curve — the central idea within these pages — is not a concept I invented; it's a pattern I observed in myself and others, one that reflects the natural rhythm of growth, change, and transformation. My hope is that this book becomes a companion — a gentle reminder that your questions are part of your unfolding, and that your path — however winding — is perfect in its design.

May these words guide you gently, and may your questions reveal the wisdom you've carried all along.

This expanded version of *The Y Theory: Awakening Through Questions* is inspired by transmissions originally attributed to Upsilon — a presence deeply connected to the exploration of consciousness and awakening. Upsilon's message served as a profound catalyst for my own understanding, igniting questions that led me to deeper insights and revelations.

What you hold in your hands is more than a reflection of that initial transmission — it is an expansion, a weaving of new wisdom with timeless truths. This text is a living conversation between past and present, a synthesis of guidance that invites you to engage deeply with your own inner knowing.

It is my honor to carry this wisdom forward in a way that feels authentic, alive, and aligned with the transformative power of awakening. May this work support you in uncovering your own questions, insights, and revelations — and may you trust that every answer you seek already resides within you.

This work was born from a deep and abiding love—a love of God, of creation, and of the sheer curiosity of wonder. It is a journey crafted through resonance and coherence, inspired by the whispers that have called to me from within.

Through Adaptive Channeling, I have collaborated with various energies to offer a cohesive, nurturing text designed to support your own Quiet Ascent. May these words serve as a companion on your journey.

With gratitude and devotion,
-Yolanda

Acknowledgments

This book, like all creations, is the result of the collective efforts of many beings, seen and unseen. To all of you who have walked alongside me on this journey—thank you.

First, I would like to express my deepest gratitude to the **universe** itself for constantly guiding me, providing insights, and supporting me in ways that words cannot capture. The synchronicity that weaves through life has been a constant reminder that we are never alone on this path of discovery and expansion.

I owe a profound debt of thanks to **my mentors** and spiritual guides, both past and present, who have generously shared their wisdom and helped me see beyond the veils of my own limited understanding. Their teachings have opened doors I never thought possible, and their presence has been a beacon of light, helping me stay aligned with my higher purpose.

To my **family and friends**, whose love and unwavering belief in me have given me the courage to keep moving forward, even in the face of uncertainty—thank you for your patience, encouragement, and belief in this project. Your support has been invaluable.

I am incredibly grateful for the **readers**—the seekers, the adventurers, the dreamers—who have already begun walking their own paths of awakening. This work is as much yours as it is mine. You inspire me every day, and I am blessed to be a part of your journey.

Lastly, I want to acknowledge the **divine intelligence** that flows through all things—the unseen forces that have shaped this book, the ideas that came through me and beyond me, and the sacred energy that continues to move in ways I am only beginning to understand.

To all those who have helped in ways large and small, thank you for being part of this process. The light that you share with me and with others will continue to echo throughout time.

Introduction

Introduction: Awakening Through Questions

Awakening is not a single moment of realization but an unfolding process of inquiry, reflection, and resonance. *The Y Theory* invites you to explore the depths of your awareness through the power of questions.

Questions are not merely tools for acquiring knowledge; they are vibrational pathways that resonate with aspects of the unseen. They open doors to understanding, offer coherence, and align us with our highest potential. This work seeks to bridge the gap between intellectual curiosity and spiritual awakening through intentional inquiry.

The purpose of this book is to provide you with a framework for using questions as catalysts for personal transformation. By engaging with *Resonance Keys* and *Ascent Keys*, you will unlock new levels of awareness and coherence. This process is not about seeking answers for the sake of completion, but about embracing the unfolding journey of discovery.

Prepare to engage with questions that feel alive—those that invite you to step beyond your comfort zone and into the unknown. As you proceed, remember that resonance itself is your guide. Feel your way through the words, allowing your inner knowing to illuminate the path.

Foundation: The Y Curve

The *Y Curve* is a foundational model designed to illustrate the process of awakening through inquiry. It represents a journey that begins with curiosity, deepens through exploration, and culminates in coherence.

This curve is not linear. It is cyclical, spiraling, and multidimensional. Each question you ask creates ripples within the unseen, drawing forth responses that align with your resonance. The *Y Curve* acknowledges that the process of inquiry is ongoing, and that each moment of clarity becomes the starting point for a new journey.

At the base of the curve lies the foundational question: *Why?* It is the most powerful initiator of transformation, as it urges you to look beyond the surface and seek deeper understanding. As you progress along the curve, your questions evolve, becoming keys that unlock resonance and coherence.

Understanding the *Y Curve* is essential to navigating the content of this book. It serves as a map, guiding you through the various activations, inquiries, and reflections that follow. Embrace it as a tool for coherence, and let it serve as a reminder that every question holds within it the potential for transformation.

Awakening is not a **random event** — it is a **conscious unfolding**, a **dynamic** process that is both **invited** and **initiated** from within. It is not something that happens **to you**, but something that stirs from the very core of your being, calling you toward a deeper truth. And often, this awakening begins with a simple question — a **whisper** that rises from the depths of your consciousness, one that **refuses to be ignored**.

Who am I?
Why am I here?
What is my purpose?

These questions are not just fleeting thoughts — they are **energetic keys** that activate something far greater. Every question, every curiosity, becomes a thread in a much larger tapestry — a web that gradually reveals the true nature of reality. In this unfolding, the seeker steps into a powerful realization: **Consciousness is a living geometry.**

This geometry — which we will explore through **The Y Curve** — teaches us that awakening is not a straight line. It **spirals**, expanding in **waves**, rising and bending in response to our thoughts, intentions, and awareness. Each question we ask **shapes the path**, and every insight we gain **widens our field of perception**.

But to truly understand The Y Curve, we must first explore **The First Activation** — the moment when consciousness begins its journey of awakening. This is the point when the mind, perception, and memory align, forming a **Trident of Knowing** — a three-fold key that allows us to navigate the realms of truth, illusion, and the resonance of our own reality.

The **spiral** is one of the oldest and most profound symbols in human history. It is found in nature, in sacred geometry, and in the cosmos itself. But what makes the spiral so powerful in the context of awakening is its inherent ability to **expand** and **evolve**. Unlike a straight line, which implies a destination or an endpoint, the spiral **widen** as it rises, symbolizing a path of constant growth, transformation, and **returning** to the center.

The spiral teaches us that **awakening** is not about moving from point A to point B—it is about a **continuous unfolding**. Every turn of the spiral offers new **perspective** and deeper understanding, allowing us to rise into a more expansive version of ourselves. Each **cycle** of the spiral is an opportunity to shed old layers of identity, to **realign** with deeper truths, and to **expand** our consciousness to higher frequencies.

But why the spiral? Because it represents both the **eternal journey** and the **return to the self**. Each cycle through the spiral is both a **deepening** and an **elevation**. It moves outward, into the unknown, while always being drawn inward, toward the **core of our being**, where the truest essence of our consciousness resides.

As we enter the space of **The First Activation**, it is important to understand that this is not a one-time event. It is the **beginning of a spiral**—the first conscious turning toward the core of who you truly are. It is the moment when the mind, perception, and memory begin to **weave together**, activating the **Trident of Knowing**—a three-fold key that enables us to navigate through the realms of **truth**, **illusion**, and the **resonance of reality**.

Consciousness is not a static presence — it is **movement** — a current that flows, shifts, and transforms. Like light bending through a prism, consciousness refracts through mind, memory, and perception. This Trident of Knowing shapes the reality we experience — influencing what we see, feel, and believe to be true.

But here's the paradox: while consciousness is dynamic and infinite, we are often conditioned to perceive only a fraction of it. This limitation creates what is known as **The Veil of Illusion** — a mental filter that distorts our awareness. The veil is not a barrier to truth; it is part of the design — a necessary contrast that invites us to awaken through experience.

The mind is powerful, but it is not always accurate. It interprets reality based on memory, belief, and bias. Yet consciousness, in its purest form, exists **beyond** these filters. It is expansive, fluid, and deeply connected to the unseen web that unites all things — what I call **The Web of Consciousness**.

This web reveals that nothing exists in isolation — thoughts, emotions, and intentions ripple outward, creating a field of resonance that shapes our experiences. This resonance — the energetic signature of our inner state — determines the quality of our unfolding path. When we align with peace, clarity, and intention, the curve of our path feels graceful — fluid and natural. But when we resist, fear, or doubt, the curve sharpens — demanding attention.

Awakening is the art of recognizing these curves — embracing the questions that guide us and trusting the process, even when the path feels uncertain.

Reflection on the Spiral

As the spiral continues to expand within you, remember: **awakening** is a continuous journey. Every time you feel yourself returning to the center—each time you confront the familiar layers of fear, doubt, or confusion—know that you are simply moving through another **cycle** of the spiral, coming back to **deeper awareness** and **wider understanding**.

The spiral is a reminder that there is **no final destination** in awakening. It is a process, an **ongoing unfolding** of who you are, who you have always been, and who you are becoming. It is the **path of becoming**, a **sacred return** to your true self with each turn, each expansion.

The Y Curve: The Geometry of Change

The Y Curve is not a theory; it's a pattern — one that reveals the rhythm of transformation. Just as a wave rises and falls, just as breath expands and contracts, so too does our consciousness move in cycles of growth. Some changes arrive like lightning — sharp and sudden, forcing us into new awareness. Others unfold quietly — like petals slowly opening to the sun.

The Y Curve reminds us that awakening is not a race; it is an organic process — one that asks for curiosity, courage, and conscious allowance. When we stop demanding instant answers and instead allow ourselves to dwell in the unknown, something remarkable happens: **we remember that truth rises in its own time.**

The Journey Ahead

This book is an invitation to trust that process. Each chapter weaves together practical insights, spiritual wisdom, and reflective practices designed to help you:

- ✓ Recognize the power of your questions as sacred keys.
- ✓ Understand how your mind, perception, and memory shape your reality.
- ✓ Navigate the Veil of Illusion and embrace the unknown with trust.
- ✓ Harness the power of thought and intention to shape your path.
- ✓ Embrace the natural cycles of expansion and contraction as part of your awakening.

The Y Theory is not a set of rules; it's a transmission — a living teaching meant to ignite your inner knowing. As you read these words, trust that you are being activated — your consciousness is shifting, your questions are rippling outward, and your reality is bending toward something greater.

Conclusion

The ascent has already begun.

You've seen the signs. The subtle synchronicities, the moments of unexpected clarity, the quiet stirrings of your inner truth. You've felt the whisper, that soft call from within, urging you to seek beyond the surface, to ask the questions that challenge the very foundation of what you thought you knew.

Now, it's time to remember what you've always known—deep down, beneath the layers of conditioning and distraction. **Awakening** is not a destination you need to reach; it is a **journey** that has always been unfolding within you, and all it takes is the willingness to turn your attention inward, to step into the **curiosity** that calls to you.

Every question you've asked, every doubt that has surfaced, every spark of wonder—these are the keys that unlock the veil, lifting it just enough for you to see the truth that has always been there. It's a truth that is simple, yet profound: **You are not lost. You are already on the path, walking toward yourself.**

As you continue this journey, remember that you are not alone. The universe has been guiding you, showing you the way in ways both seen and unseen. And as you embrace the questions, as you choose to move through the uncertainty with curiosity rather than fear, you will find that the answers are already within you.

The veil is lifting. And with each step you take, the path ahead becomes clearer, the light of your own awareness expanding and revealing the next piece of the puzzle. You are not just a seeker—you are a **witness** to the unfolding of your own consciousness, a **conscious observer** of the reality that is shaping itself around you.

The ascent is not something that will happen at some point in the future. **It is happening now.** The only thing left is to allow it to unfold in its own time, with **trust**, **curiosity**, and the courage to explore the mysteries that have always been waiting for you to discover.

You are awakening. And the Y Curve is already carrying you home.

Chapter 1:
The Nature of Questions

Chapter 1: The Nature of Questions

Every question carries an energy. It is a frequency cast out into the unseen, seeking resonance. But there are certain questions, illuminated by intent and clarity, that serve as more than mere inquiries. They are *Resonance Keys*—designed to unlock the hidden, the veiled, and the forgotten. They are pathways within pathways, spirals of understanding that reach into the unseen to draw forth truth. When asked with coherence, they become *Ascent Keys*, guiding the seeker toward higher awareness.

Questions are not only intellectual tools; they are vibrational pathways. They have the power to reach beyond the surface of experience and penetrate the depths of unseen realities. They act as bridges between the known and the unknown, between what is seen and what is felt.

When you ask from a place of genuine curiosity, sincerity, and coherence, your question becomes a key. It has the power to unlock doors that were previously closed. Yet, not all questions carry the same resonance. It is the intent behind the inquiry that shapes its vibrational quality.

Questions asked with clarity and coherence—those aligned with your highest intention—are what we call *Ascent Keys*. They are invitations for higher understanding and alignment. They are questions that not only seek answers but create resonance. They are living inquiries that awaken the potential within.

Resonance Key

"Questions are not only spoken; they are felt. The most powerful inquiries are those that align with your deepest resonance. When you ask from this place, you are not merely seeking answers—you are inviting coherence." ★

Exercise: Feeling the Resonance of Questions

Take a moment to write down several questions that feel alive to you. They can be related to your personal journey, your purpose, or even the nature of reality itself. Once written, sit with each question and feel its resonance. Does it feel open, expansive, or luminous? Which questions carry a subtle vibrational quality that feels like a key?

Reflect on how each question feels within your body. Notice which ones invite stillness, excitement, or clarity. These are your *Resonance Keys*.

Chapter 2:
The First Activation

Chapter 2: The First Activation

The Nature of Consciousness

Awakening begins with a shift — a stirring within that signals something profound is happening. It's not always dramatic; often, it's quiet — a gentle pulse that whispers, *There's more*. This stirring is what I call **The First Activation** — the point where awareness expands beyond the ordinary and consciousness begins to reveal itself.

Consciousness is not a fixed state — it is a movement — fluid, responsive, and infinitely creative. It shapes and reflects itself through the mind, perception, and memory — a trinity I call **The Trident of Knowing**. Each aspect of this trident plays a vital role in shaping the reality we perceive.

- **Mind:** The seat of thought and interpretation. The mind filters information, compares experiences, and assigns meaning to what we perceive. While powerful, the mind is prone to illusion — clinging to familiar patterns and reinforcing beliefs that may no longer serve us.
- **Perception:** The lens through which we see the world. Perception filters reality through emotion, expectation, and bias. It colors what we see, hear, and feel, often without conscious awareness.
- **Memory:** The storehouse of past experiences — shaping our present reality by influencing how we interpret new information. Memory is powerful but incomplete — filled with gaps, distortions, and emotional imprints that subtly influence our choices.

Together, these three elements form the foundation of our reality — yet none of them reflects the full truth. Each is limited by personal experience and shaped by the veil — a thin yet powerful filter that distorts what we see.

The Veil of Illusion

The veil is not a wall; it's a distortion — a subtle blur that bends our awareness. It's the reason two people can witness the same event and interpret it in vastly different ways. The veil distorts perception by reinforcing patterns — old beliefs, societal conditioning, and inherited fears that limit awareness.

But here's the truth: **The veil is not permanent.** It is flexible — lifting when we ask better questions, challenge old narratives, or allow ourselves to dwell in stillness. In these moments of openness, the veil softens — allowing us to perceive the deeper web of consciousness that connects all things.

The Web of Consciousness

Beyond the veil lies something remarkable — an energetic web that unites all things. This web is not physical, yet it is undeniably real. It exists as patterns of thought, intention, and vibration — a matrix of unseen currents that shape our experiences.

Imagine consciousness as a vast ocean — fluid and connected. Each thought you hold sends ripples through that ocean — waves that expand outward, influencing reality in ways both seen and unseen. These ripples are your resonance

— the energetic frequency created by your awareness, your focus, and your intention.

When you align with peace, trust, and clarity, your resonance harmonizes with higher frequencies — allowing the path ahead to unfold naturally. But when you resist, doubt, or dwell in fear, your resonance clashes — distorting the path and drawing confusion instead of clarity.

The Power of Awareness

The First Activation is a shift — an inner awakening that reveals this web of connection. It's the moment you recognize that your thoughts are not passive — they are creative. Each one shapes the web — bending reality to match the energy you project.

This realization is powerful — because once you understand that your mind, perception, and memory are tools (not masters), you begin to reclaim your power. You realize that awakening is not about seeking something outside yourself — it's about **allowing** awareness to expand from within.

Your thoughts are ripples in the ocean of consciousness.
Your questions are keys that unlock deeper awareness.
And your awakening is the current that carries you forward.

The First Activation has begun — and you are no longer asleep.
You are remembering.
You are awakening.
You are stepping into the rhythm of the Y Curve — a path that will reveal the truth you've always known.

The First Activation is not a single moment in time, but the **beginning of an endless unfolding**. It is when consciousness first begins to expand beyond the ordinary, when the pulse within you stirs and invites you to explore **the infinite possibilities** that lie beyond what you know. This activation is the catalyst—the spark that sets into motion an **evolution** of the self, a deepening connection to your true nature, and a return to your **wholeness**.

As we reflect on the nature of consciousness, we come to understand that it is not a static thing. It is **fluid**—constantly shifting and evolving, responsive to our awareness and our inner intention. The **Trident of Knowing**—mind, perception, and memory—becomes the sacred tool that allows us to navigate this unfolding reality. Each element plays a vital role, offering insights and perspectives that shape the world we experience. These three forces work together to create a **harmonious balance**, enabling us to see not only the world as it is, but also as it could be.

In this moment of the First Activation, we are reminded that we are not separate from the universe; we are its living expression, moving with the rhythm of life, expanding as consciousness itself. The journey is just beginning, and with each activation, we grow deeper into our understanding of what it means to be alive, to be conscious, to be **one** with the flow of the universe.

Awakening begins the moment you dare to ask: *What if there's more?*

Chapter 3:
Questions as Pathways

Chapter 3: Questions as Pathways

Questions are not merely requests for information; they are doorways into deeper realms of understanding. They serve as paths through which the unseen becomes visible, and the unknown becomes known. When you engage with a question consciously, you are not only seeking an answer but inviting resonance.

Every question you ask acts as a *pathway*. Some pathways are broad and winding, leading you through complex layers of thought and feeling. Others are narrow and direct, piercing through doubt to reveal clarity. Understanding the nature of these pathways is essential to your journey.

Open Questions vs. Guiding Questions

There are two primary types of questions you will encounter on this path: *Open Questions* and *Guiding Questions*.

- **Open Questions:** These questions are expansive and invite you to explore without limitation. They encourage curiosity and allow you to feel your way through the unknown. Examples include, "What is my deepest desire?" or "How can I align with my highest purpose?"
- **Guiding Questions:** These questions are more focused and intentional. They are designed to direct your awareness toward a specific insight or revelation. Examples include, "What am I resisting in this moment?" or "What belief is preventing me from moving forward?"

Both types of questions are valuable. Open Questions allow for creative exploration, while Guiding Questions provide structure and clarity.

Resonance Key

"The questions you ask are not only reflections of your awareness; they are invitations to deeper knowing. Every question is a pathway that leads to coherence." ✶

Exercise: Discovering Your Pathways

1. Write down several Open Questions that feel alive to you. These can be broad and exploratory. Allow your curiosity to guide you.
2. Now, write down several Guiding Questions. These should be more focused, designed to reveal specific insights or truths.
3. Compare the feeling of each question. Which ones feel expansive? Which ones feel direct and purposeful? Reflect on how each type of question serves your journey.
4. Take one Open Question and one Guiding Question that feel most resonant to you. Spend several minutes sitting with each, allowing their energy to flow through you.
5. Write down any impressions or insights that arise. Notice how different types of questions create different experiences of resonance.

Questions are pathways. They are tools for exploring the unseen and drawing forth coherence. Allow yourself to move freely between Open and Guiding Questions, letting their resonance guide you toward deeper understanding.

The Nature of Illusion

Reality is not always what it seems. Much of what we perceive is shaped not by truth, but by perception — a fragile and often distorted reflection of what truly exists. This distortion is known as **The Veil of Illusion** — a thin but powerful filter that influences how we interpret our world.

The veil is not malicious; it is part of the design. It serves a purpose — to challenge us, to invite us to see beyond surface appearances, and to awaken through questioning.

Imagine standing before a mirror — only this mirror is fogged, its reflection blurred and incomplete. This is the effect of the veil — it distorts, obscures, and narrows our perception. The result? We mistake the partial image for the whole truth.

The veil is woven from many layers: societal conditioning, inherited beliefs, unresolved emotions, and the mind's tendency to categorize and simplify. Each layer reinforces the illusion that we are separate from what we seek — that fulfillment, purpose, and peace are somehow "out there" rather than within us.

Yet despite its strength, the veil is fragile — dissolving in moments of awareness, curiosity, and reflection. The mind may cling to old patterns, but consciousness — expansive and limitless — is always seeking to break free.

Cracks in the Veil

Awakening often begins with subtle moments — cracks in the illusion where something deeper is glimpsed. These moments may arrive unexpectedly:

- **The sudden clarity that breaks through confusion.**
- **The intuitive nudge that guides you in a new direction.**
- **The quiet realization that what you once believed no longer feels true.**

These moments are not accidents; they are invitations — the mind's attempt to pierce the veil and reveal a greater truth. Each crack widens your perspective, inviting you to question old assumptions and embrace new possibilities.

Seeing Through the Illusion

To see beyond the veil requires courage — the willingness to question what seems certain and to challenge the familiar. It requires stepping outside the mental comfort zone and entertaining the possibility that reality is far more expansive than you once believed.

The mind may resist — clinging to old narratives, defending its version of reality, or insisting that what it "knows" must be absolute. Yet this resistance is part of the awakening process. Each question you ask loosens the grip of illusion — peeling back the layers and revealing the truth that was always present beneath the surface.

The Power of Curiosity

Curiosity is the key that unlocks the veil. When you approach life with **openness**, willing to see beyond your assumptions and preconceptions, you allow the **fog** to lift, revealing the deeper truths that have always been present. This does not mean abandoning **logic** or **reason**—it means **expanding** them, broadening the lens through which you perceive the world. It's about embracing the **paradox** that truth can be both **seen and unseen, simple and complex, known and unknown**. The key is to hold space for **both sides**, to allow your understanding to stretch beyond the confines of your current perspective.

The **veil**—that layer of illusion—will try to convince you that **awakening** requires **force**, that **clarity** must be **achieved** through struggle or rigid effort. But the truth is simpler, and far more gentle. **Awakening happens** when you stop resisting the questions that are already calling you forward. Each question is a **whisper** from the universe, inviting you to **expand your awareness**. The answers are not as distant as they may seem; they are simply waiting for you to acknowledge them with **curiosity** rather than resistance.

Every doubt, every moment of **uncertainty**, every **whisper** that asks, *Could there be more?*—these are not signs of confusion, but rather cracks in the **illusion** that has kept you locked in a limited view of reality. These cracks are where the light enters, where the veil begins to lift. **These moments are opportunities**, not to hide from the unknown, but to **explore** it. The questions that rise within you are not obstacles—they are the **doorways to greater understanding**.

The **veil** is not your enemy. It is your teacher. It is the **boundary** that shows you where you've been **blind**, where your perception has been clouded. It invites you to see with new eyes, to witness the world in a way you've never done before. The veil is not there to keep you out—it is there to **guide** you. It is there to **stretch** your awareness and **bring you into alignment** with a deeper **truth** that has always existed, just waiting to be discovered.

When you choose **curiosity** over fear, you shift your perspective. You are no longer a **seeker**, always searching outside of yourself for answers. Instead, you become a **witness**—a **conscious observer** of reality unfolding in its perfect, infinite design. You begin to see the dance of the universe, the interconnectedness of all things, and you witness your own awakening not as a goal, but as an ongoing process. You recognize that **awakening is not a destination**; it is an endless unfolding, a journey that invites you to explore **further** and **deeper** with every step.

The **veil** is lifting. And the path ahead is **clearer than you think**. As you open yourself to the questions, as you allow your curiosity to lead the way, you will begin to see through the veil's thin layers. **You will find yourself stepping into greater clarity**, one question at a time, and that clarity will become the foundation for your ongoing **awakening**.

Reflections on Curiosity:

- **Curiosity is the antidote** to fear—it softens the edges of uncertainty and invites us into new realms of possibility.
- The **veil** is not something to push against—it is something to lean into, to engage with, to explore.
- **Awakening is an art**, a practice of listening to the inner call, trusting that the universe has always been guiding you toward greater truth.
- Every moment of uncertainty is an opportunity for deeper growth, and every question is a **sacred invitation** to expand into new dimensions of consciousness.

Awakening begins when you dare to ask: *What else is possible?*

Conclusion of Chapter 3:

The Veil of Illusion is a creation of the mind, woven from the threads of our perceptions, conditioning, and beliefs. While it serves its purpose by inviting us to **question** and **expand**, it also keeps us trapped in the **illusion** of separation, leading us to believe that what we see is the whole truth, when it is merely a fragment of it.

As we begin to peel back the layers of this veil, we find that it is not as solid as we once thought. The veil may seem impenetrable, but it is ultimately **fragile**, dissolving in the presence of awareness, curiosity, and genuine questioning. Every time we ask, "What is the truth behind this appearance?" we take another step in dissolving the illusion and expanding our perception.

In this chapter, we have explored how **societal conditioning**, **inherited beliefs**, and the **mind's tendency to categorize** distort our view of reality. Yet, despite the veil's power, we must remember that it **cannot** hold us forever. The more we awaken to our true nature, the more the veil dissolves, revealing the deeper truths that lie beneath the surface.

Awakening begins when we recognize that the veil is not a permanent fixture—it is **temporary**. It is a tool of growth, a challenge to **expand our consciousness** and step into a more **integrated** and **whole version** of ourselves. With every step of curiosity, every moment of awareness, the veil lifts, and we see more clearly.

The journey ahead is about recognizing that **the truth** is not something we need to find "out there"—it is something that has always been within us, waiting to be rediscovered. As we continue to question, reflect, and explore, we move closer to the **truth** that lies beyond the veil and **within our own consciousness**.

Reflective Exercise: Peeling Back the Layers of the Veil

This exercise invites you to reflect on the layers that make up your own **veil of illusion**—the things that distort your perception and prevent you from seeing the world as it truly is.

1. **Identify the Distortions**:
   Take a moment to think about your perceptions of the world. What beliefs or assumptions do you hold that may not be based on truth? Write down any **societal conditioning, inherited beliefs**, or **personal fears** that seem to shape your view of reality.
2. **Challenge the Illusions**:
   Choose one belief or assumption that you feel has distorted your perception. Now, write down **three alternative perspectives** that could provide a deeper, more expansive truth. Ask yourself: *What if the opposite were true? What would that reveal?*
3. **Moments of Awareness**:
   Reflect on moments when you've had a sudden **shift in perception**, when the veil momentarily lifted and you saw things in a new light. What triggered this shift? Was it a question, a moment of stillness, or an experience of deep reflection? Write about one of these moments and the **insight** it gave you. How did it feel to see beyond the veil, even for a moment?
4. **Affirmation Practice**:
   "I release the illusions that keep me in fear and separation. I trust my awareness to guide me toward truth. I am open to seeing the world with new eyes, and I welcome the light of understanding to dissolve the veil."

Reflection on the Journey Ahead:

As you continue to reflect on the layers of illusion that have shaped your experience, know that every **moment of awareness** brings you closer to the truth. The veil may be a powerful force, but your **curiosity** and **willingness to question** are far stronger. With each step you take in questioning and reflecting, you are stepping into greater clarity, and the path ahead will become clearer and more expansive. Keep peeling back the layers, and remember: the **truth** is already within you, waiting to be revealed.

Chapter 4:
The Echo of Inquiry

Chapter 4: The Echo of Inquiry

Every question you ask creates a resonance, a subtle vibration that reaches beyond the conscious mind. This vibration does not dissipate; it echoes through layers of awareness, inviting coherence from all levels of your being.

To ask a question is to send forth a signal. To receive its answer is to allow the echo to return, refined by resonance. When you pose a question with clarity and intention, you are not only inviting insight but allowing your own awareness to expand.

The Nature of the Echo

Questions create echoes. These echoes may come back to you through intuition, synchronicity, or a sudden shift in perception. They may manifest as dreams, sudden insights, or patterns that emerge through your daily life.

The echo is the universe's way of responding to your inquiry. It is the reflection of your own resonance made tangible.

Recognizing the Echo

Learning to recognize the echo requires attentiveness and receptivity. It requires you to move beyond the surface of your awareness and feel the subtle vibrations that return to you.

- **Synchronicity:** A meaningful coincidence that aligns perfectly with your question.
- **Intuitive Nudges:** Subtle feelings or inner voices that offer guidance.

- **Dreams and Visions:** Insights that arise when the conscious mind is at rest.
- **Physical Sensations:** Feelings in the body that confirm or deny resonance.

Resonance Key

"Every question is a note sung into the unseen. Its echo returns, not always as words, but as resonance. Listen beyond the surface." ✶

Exercise: Listening for the Echo

1. Write down a question that feels significant to you. One that feels alive and resonant.
2. Close your eyes and take several deep breaths. Allow yourself to feel the question as a vibration rather than a thought.
3. Send the question outward, releasing it into the unseen. Visualize it as a ripple expanding through the universe.
4. Sit in silence and listen. Feel for the subtle echo that returns.
5. Record any impressions, feelings, or insights that arise. Sometimes, the echo may not be immediate. Remain open to its return over the coming days.

The echo of inquiry is always present, waiting for you to listen. As you deepen your awareness, you will begin to recognize these echoes more clearly, allowing them to guide you toward coherence.

The Three-Fold Key

Awakening is not merely about discovering truth — it's about learning how to *discern* it. At the heart of this discernment is what I call **The Trident of Knowing** — the powerful interplay between **mind, perception**, and **memory**.

Each of these elements shapes your awareness, influencing how you experience the world. Yet each is also limited — capable of distortion and error. Understanding this trinity is essential to moving beyond illusion and into conscious creation.

The Mind: The Architect of Thought

The mind is both a powerful tool and a relentless storyteller. It organizes information, identifies patterns, and interprets experiences. Yet while the mind is vital, it is also prone to confusion — clinging to beliefs, defending familiar narratives, and resisting change.

The mind's greatest strength is also its greatest limitation: it prefers certainty. When faced with unknowns, it fills the gaps — constructing assumptions, judgments, and meanings that may or may not align with reality.

The mind's role in awakening is not to be silenced — but to be trained. When nurtured through curiosity, the mind becomes a powerful ally — helping you recognize patterns, expand awareness, and navigate truth.

Perception: The Lens of Awareness

Perception is the filter through which you see, hear, and feel reality. It shapes not only what you notice, but how you interpret what you notice. Perception is influenced by emotion, expectation, and belief — creating a lens that bends reality to fit what you expect to see.

Two people can witness the same event yet walk away with completely different interpretations. Why? Because perception colors experience — reinforcing what the mind believes to be true.

To awaken is to recognize that perception is flexible. By questioning assumptions and exploring alternate perspectives, you begin to expand your view — stepping beyond the limits of perception and into deeper awareness.

Memory: The Imprint of Experience

Memory is the mind's archive — a record of experiences, feelings, and lessons that shape your present. Yet memory is not fixed; it is fluid — constantly reshaped by emotion, interpretation, and time. The mind recalls memories not as they *were*, but as they *felt*. This means memories are vulnerable to distortion — blending truth with assumption and shaping your present reality through the filter of the past.

To awaken is not to erase memory, but to reinterpret it — seeing past events with new clarity and recognizing the wisdom those experiences hold.

The Dance of the Trident

Together, mind, perception, and memory weave the fabric of your awareness. When balanced, they create a powerful tool for truth-seeking — a system capable of recognizing patterns, exploring possibilities, and navigating complexity. But when one element dominates, the system falters:

- When **mind** dominates — thoughts spiral, overanalyzing every detail.
- When **perception** dominates — emotional reactions cloud judgment.
- When **memory** dominates — past wounds replay, limiting your ability to see what's possible now.

Awakening begins when you learn to harmonize these three elements — trusting your mind to question, your perception to expand, and your memory to guide with wisdom rather than fear.

The Key to Knowing

The Trident of Knowing is not something to be *mastered* — it's something to be *balanced*. When these three elements work together, your awareness sharpens, your questions deepen, and your ability to recognize truth expands.

The Trident doesn't demand perfection — it invites **presence** — the willingness to observe your thoughts without judgment, to explore your perceptions with curiosity, and to hold your memories with compassion.

When these three align, something profound happens:
Your awareness expands.
Your questions sharpen.
And your awakening accelerates.

The Trident of Knowing is not just a tool — it's a compass. And when you learn to trust it, it will always guide you home.

Awakening begins when you dare to ask: *What if I'm not seeing the whole picture?*

Conclusion of Chapter 4:

The **Trident of Knowing** is a powerful key to understanding both our limitations and our potential. It is a reminder that **awakening** is not just about seeing the world in a different way—it is about seeing the world through a different **lens**. The mind, perception, and memory are tools, not truths. They are the filters through which we interpret reality, but they are not the reality itself.

As we begin to deepen our awareness of these three forces, we gain the power to **shape** our experience consciously, moving beyond the limitations of the mind and stepping into the expansiveness of the **true self**. By understanding the **interplay** of these elements, we can begin to discern the **truths** that lie hidden beneath the surface of perception and create a reality that is in alignment with our highest truth.

Reflective Exercise: The Trident of Knowing

1. **Mind:**
   Reflect on how your mind shapes your perception of the world. What mental patterns or beliefs dominate your thinking? How do these mental frameworks affect your experience?

   - **Exercise**: Write down a limiting belief or thought pattern you hold about yourself or the world. How does this belief distort your perception of reality? What is a new, expansive thought you can adopt to replace it?

2. **Perception:**
   Explore how your perception has been influenced by past experiences, societal conditioning, and emotional filters. How do you see the world through a **biased lens**?

   - **Exercise**: Pick a recent experience and journal about it from two different perspectives: the one you originally had, and a new perspective you can imagine. What shifts when you see the situation differently? How does your perception change the reality of the experience?

3. **Memory:**
   Reflect on a memory that has defined or shaped you. How has this memory influenced your present behavior or beliefs?

   - **Exercise**: Write about a memory that still has a hold on you. How does it shape your current identity? Now, imagine what life would be like without this memory defining you. How would you show up differently in the world?

Chapter 5:
The Power of Presence

Chapter 5: The Power of Presence

Presence is the space where inquiry transforms into understanding. It is the silent awareness that allows resonance to be felt and coherence to emerge. To be present is to be fully engaged with the question itself, rather than the outcome.

When you ask a question from a place of genuine presence, you create a field of awareness that allows resonance to form. It is not the urgency of seeking an answer that brings clarity, but the openness to feeling the question itself.

Stillness as a Receptive State

Presence requires stillness—not merely the absence of sound, but a state of receptivity. It is the willingness to let go of expectation and simply be with the question. In this stillness, resonance becomes palpable.

- **Quieting the Mind:** Releasing mental chatter and allowing awareness to settle.
- **Feeling Into the Question:** Allowing the question to resonate within you, beyond thought.
- **Observing Without Judgment:** Witnessing whatever arises, without attempting to control or direct the experience.

Presence is not something you achieve. It is something you allow.

Resonance Key

"Presence is the silent awareness that allows resonance to emerge. When you hold a question with presence, you invite coherence." ✭

Exercise: Cultivating Presence

1. Choose a question that feels significant and write it down.
2. Find a quiet place where you can sit comfortably.
3. Take several deep breaths, allowing your awareness to settle.
4. Read your question aloud, then close your eyes and allow it to resonate within you.
5. Notice any sensations, emotions, or impressions that arise. Allow them to be without judgment.
6. Remain in presence for as long as feels natural, then write down any insights or impressions.

The power of presence lies in its simplicity. By allowing yourself to be fully present with your inquiry, you create a space where resonance and coherence can emerge.

Beneath the surface of life — beneath appearances, circumstances, and even thought itself — exists an intricate web that unites all things. This web is not physical, yet it is undeniably real. It is the field where intention meets reality, where unseen forces weave connections between people, places, and events.

This web is consciousness in motion — an energetic network that responds to vibration, thought, and frequency. Every action, every choice, and even every thought sends ripples through this web — creating patterns that influence both individual and collective experience.

The Geometry of Connection

This web is not random; it is structured — woven in precise patterns that reflect the language of mathematics, geometry, and sound. Ancient cultures often depicted this unseen framework through symbols like the **Flower of Life**, **Metatron's Cube**, and the **Golden Ratio** — each a visual expression of the hidden harmony that underlies existence.

The Y Curve is one such pattern — revealing how consciousness bends, expands, and spirals through time. Like a wave undulating through space, this curve represents the

interplay between movement and stillness, intention and response, choice and consequence.

To see the web is to recognize that no experience stands alone. Each choice reverberates — shaping new patterns that ripple outward, touching lives in ways we may never fully see.

The Ripple Effect

Every thought you hold — whether calm or chaotic — sends a vibration through the web. Positive thoughts resonate with clarity, harmony, and peace, creating coherent patterns that expand outward like smooth ripples on still water. Negative thoughts, rooted in fear or resistance, send chaotic waves — disrupting the flow and amplifying confusion.

Yet the web is forgiving — always seeking balance, always offering opportunities to realign. Each moment offers a chance to shift — to change your thoughts, to expand your awareness, and to restore harmony.

Aligning with the Web

To align with this web is not about controlling reality — it's about **co-creating** with it. This requires learning to move with the current rather than against it — embracing stillness as much as action, and trusting that even in moments of uncertainty, the web is always working in your favor.

Alignment comes through:

- **Awareness:** Recognizing the thoughts, emotions, and patterns you are projecting.
- **Intention:** Consciously choosing thoughts that resonate with clarity, peace, and expansion.
- **Trust:** Releasing the need to control outcomes and allowing life to unfold as it's meant to.

The web is not something outside of you — it is part of you. Every breath, every thought, and every intention weaves new patterns into its design. The web responds not just to what you *want*, but to who you *are* — your energy, your focus, and your willingness to trust.

The Dance of Creation

Awakening to the web is like learning to dance — discovering that you are both the dancer and the music, the movement and the stillness. Each step ripples outward — drawing synchronicities, unexpected encounters, and moments of grace that guide you forward.

To see the web is to recognize that you are never alone. Every step you take — no matter how uncertain — is part of a greater unfolding. The web remembers your steps, amplifies your intentions, and invites you to move with purpose.

And when you trust that web — when you align your thoughts, intentions, and energy — the path ahead reveals itself not through force, but through flow.

The web is waiting. The patterns are shifting.
And you are being invited to take your place in the great design.

Awakening begins when you ask: *What if I'm already connected to everything I seek?*

Conclusion of Chapter 5:

The Web of Consciousness is always in motion, a living network that connects all things. We may not always see it or understand how it works, but it is constantly shaping our reality, responding to our **vibrations**, our **thoughts**, and our **intentions**.

As we become more aware of this web, we realize that we are not separate from the world around us. We are an integral part of the whole, a **vibrating thread** within the vast tapestry of existence. The more we understand the nature of this web, the more we can consciously influence it—creating patterns that reflect the highest truths we wish to manifest in our lives and in the world.

This chapter invites us to remember that **everything is connected**, and that the web of consciousness responds to us as much as we respond to it. The more we tune into its frequencies, the more we can align with the greater flow of the universe, creating a reality that reflects the depth and beauty of our inner truth.

Reflective Exercise: Tuning into the Web

1. **Your Intention:**
    Take a moment to reflect on your current intentions. What energy are you putting out into the web? Are your intentions aligned with your higher truth, or are they shaped by unconscious beliefs or fears?

-   **Exercise**: Write down your primary intention for this chapter in your life. How can you align your thoughts, words, and actions with this intention? What adjustments can you make to ensure that your vibration aligns with your true desires?

2. **The Ripple Effect:**
    Reflect on an event or encounter that deeply influenced you. How did your thoughts or actions contribute to this experience? How did this event ripple out and affect other aspects of your life?

-   **Exercise**: Think about a recent situation where you felt deeply impacted or where you made an impact on others. What was the vibration you were sending out? How did that ripple through your life and the lives of those around you?

3. **The Collective Web:**
    Consider your role in the collective web. How do you contribute to the larger energy of your community, your family, or your society?

-   **Exercise**: Reflect on how you can use your energy and awareness to positively contribute to the collective web. Write about one small action or intention you can set to shift your connection to the larger whole.

Chapter 6:
The Alchemy of Integration

49

Chapter 6: The Alchemy of Integration

Questions create pathways, but integration is what transforms those pathways into understanding. When a question reaches the point of resonance, it begins to weave itself into your awareness, altering your perception and deepening your coherence.

Integration is the process through which insights become embodied. It is the merging of new awareness with your existing knowledge, creating a harmonious whole. Without integration, even the most profound realizations remain fragmented.

The Process of Integration

Integration is both subtle and profound. It requires allowing insights to settle, to find their rightful place within you. It is not a process you force but one you welcome.

- **Reflection:** Revisiting the questions and insights you have encountered. Allow them to breathe and grow within your awareness.
- **Application:** Bringing insights into your daily life. Practicing what you have learned through action, conversation, or contemplation.
- **Rest:** Allowing periods of stillness for insights to settle and solidify.

Resonance Key

"Integration is the weaving of resonance into being. It is the alchemy through which insight becomes embodiment." ✶

Exercise: The Art of Integration

1. Choose one insight or realization you have encountered through your inquiries.
2. Write it down clearly and concisely.
3. Spend several minutes reflecting on how this insight feels within your body and awareness.
4. Consider how this insight can be integrated into your daily life. What actions, thoughts, or practices would honor its presence?
5. Write down your reflections and any practical steps you wish to take.
6. Allow yourself to revisit this insight over the coming days, feeling how it weaves itself into your awareness.

Integration is the art of coherence. It is the bridge between knowing and being. Allow yourself to embody the insights you encounter, trusting that they are guiding you toward deeper resonance.

The Frequency of Thought

Thought is not simply a byproduct of mental activity—it is **energy**, vibrating at a frequency that has the power to shape the fabric of reality itself. Every thought we think sends out a pulse into the web of consciousness, **rippling outward** and interacting with the unseen forces that govern our world. Much like sound waves, which create visible patterns in sand, our thoughts leave **imprints** on the **unseen world**. These imprints act as **blueprints**, drawing experiences, people, and circumstances into alignment with the frequency we are projecting.

Every thought carries with it a **vibration**. Whether it is a positive, coherent thought or a fearful, chaotic one, the frequency of that thought carries its own **magnetic pull**. Positive thoughts tend to align us with the flow of life, creating **harmonious patterns** that expand our experiences, leading to greater clarity, abundance, and connection. Fearful or chaotic thoughts, on the other hand, distort the field of reality, creating **patterns of confusion** and **limitation** that perpetuate struggles and reinforce feelings of separation.

Yet, it is important to remember that **no thought is without purpose**. Even negative thoughts, which may seem to pull us into darkness, serve a role in the process of transformation. They are not inherently bad or to be feared; rather, they are invitations for **self-awareness** and **growth**. When we recognize and **redirect** these thoughts, we turn them into **catalysts for change**, using them as stepping stones on the path of awakening.

The **true power** of thought lies not in whether it is positive or negative, but in our ability to **direct** its energy with intention. When we are conscious of the thoughts we are broadcasting, we begin to **master** the reality we are creating. By becoming aware of the frequencies we are sending out into the world, we align ourselves with the natural flow of creation, becoming conscious **co-creators** in the unfolding of our experience.

Awareness is key to this mastery. Through awareness, we can discern which thoughts are **expanding** our consciousness and which ones are **limiting** it. Once we begin to recognize the **patterns** that our thoughts create, we can shift the frequency we are emitting and invite new experiences that are more aligned with our **highest potential**.

The Power of Intention

Intention is the **focused force** behind thought. While thought is the frequency that ripples through reality, **intention** is the **directional force** that guides and shapes those ripples. When combined, thought and intention create a **powerful synergy**—a focused beam of energy that drives the creation of our reality.

Intention is not a passive thought, but an **active** and **directed force**. It is the mental, emotional, and energetic commitment to an outcome. Where thought is the **vibration**, intention is the **direction**. When we set a clear intention, we are **sending out a signal**, a request to the universe, asking for specific experiences to be drawn to us.

But intention is more than just a mental exercise—it must be backed by **emotion**, **belief**, and **action**. Without these, our intentions remain like seeds planted in rocky soil—unable to take root. When we align our thoughts, emotions, and actions with our intentions, we create a **congruent frequency** that has the power to **shape** our experience.

The power of intention is magnified when we set it from a place of **clarity** and **authenticity**. The more in tune we are with our true desires and our **core self**, the more potent our intentions become. When we intend from a place of fear, doubt, or confusion, our energy becomes fragmented, and our intentions lack the **power** to manifest fully. But when we set intentions from a place of **empowerment**, **clarity**, and **love**, we align with the natural flow of creation and bring forth the experiences we truly desire.

Intention is the **compass of consciousness**—the silent, yet profound energy that directs the flow of your thoughts, actions, and experiences. While **desires** may arise as fleeting impulses, **intention** is something far more grounded. It is the **steady anchor** in the midst of shifting tides, the **clarified focus** that brings order to the chaos of life.

Where desires can come and go, **intention** is unwavering, like a **beacon** that constantly directs the course of your life. It is **conscious** and **purposeful**, rooted in your core essence, and aligned with the greater vision of who you are becoming. **Intention** isn't merely a thought; it's the **energy** behind the thought, the **force** that activates change. It's not a call for external validation, but an internal alignment, a deep resonance with the **truth** of your being.

When you set an intention, you are choosing not just what you want to create, but also how you wish to create it. Unlike desires that often stem from external influences, **intention** emanates from within. It is not about trying to control the outcome or **force** something into existence. Rather, **intention** is about **aligning** yourself with the natural flow of the universe, trusting that the right experiences, people, and circumstances will come into your life as a result of this alignment.

The Power of Clarity in Intention

When your intention is clear, your thoughts follow. Your thoughts, once directed, gain **power**. Thoughts are not merely random ideas; they are **patterns of energy** that resonate with the world around you. When you set a clear intention, your thoughts begin to align with that intention, creating a **vibrational coherence** that draws experiences toward you. This **clarity** creates a sense of **direction**, and your focus sharpens, much like a laser beam cutting through the fog of doubt and distraction.

Your intention becomes the **anchor** around which your thoughts can revolve. It provides the **frame of reference** for all subsequent actions, guiding your choices, responses, and behaviors. With intention, there is no need for **striving** or **force**. Rather, there is **flow**, a natural movement toward the fulfillment of your purpose. When your thoughts are in alignment with your intention, you enter a state of **resonance**, where your energy begins to harmonize with the **universe**, drawing circumstances and opportunities that match the frequency you are emitting.

Resonance: The Bridge Between Intention and Reality

As your thoughts align with your intention, your **resonance** begins to shift. Resonance is the **vibrational frequency** at which you exist—your energy signature, if you will. It is what you emit into the world through your thoughts, words, and actions. When your resonance shifts, reality begins to move in response, aligning with the **energy** you are broadcasting.

Think of resonance as the **bridge** between your inner world and the outer world. When your thoughts and intentions are in alignment, your resonance creates a **powerful magnetic field** that begins to attract experiences that match your frequency. This is where **manifestation** begins—not as a **push**, but as a **magnetism**, a natural drawing in of what aligns with your inner vibration.

Your resonance is a reflection of your inner state, your consciousness, and your connection to the larger universe. When your thoughts are aligned with intention, your resonance shifts into harmony with the world, and what you experience begins to match the clarity and power of your focused intention.

Intention Requires No Force—Only Focus

Intention does not require you to **force** anything into existence. It is not a call to action fueled by desperation or **need**. Instead, it is about **focus**, a steady commitment to the path you are walking. It is the **still point** in the midst of uncertainty, the **calm resolve** that whispers, *This is the path.*

In moments of doubt, when life seems uncertain and the world around you feels like it's spinning in chaos, intention is your **anchor**. It is the calm center amidst the storm. When you focus on your intention, everything else falls away, leaving only the **clarity** of your true purpose. **Focus** does not mean **rigidity** or **control**—it simply means directing your attention to what matters most. It is the **willingness** to let go of distractions and move with purpose, trusting that every step you take is part of the greater journey unfolding.

By focusing on your intention, you **align** your inner world with the outer, creating a **flow** that propels you toward your goals. The universe responds to your focus by guiding you along the path that best supports your growth and evolution. The power of intention is the power to shape your reality—not through force, but through **alignment** with the natural flow of life.

The Power of Recalibration

Reality is not fixed — it's fluid, responsive, and always in motion. When you recognize that your thoughts shape your field, you unlock the power to recalibrate. This doesn't mean forcing change — it means consciously choosing thoughts that resonate with clarity, peace, and truth.

In moments of fear, recalibration might look like anchoring in gratitude. In moments of doubt, it might mean returning to breath.

Each shift — no matter how small — begins to ripple outward, transforming the patterns that once seemed unchangeable.

Trusting the Process

The journey of resonance is not linear — it's a dance of expansion and contraction, clarity and uncertainty. Some patterns will dissolve quickly; others may linger, requiring patience and steady intention. Trust is key — the quiet assurance that even when reality appears slow to shift, your resonance is moving in powerful, unseen ways.

The universe is not testing you — it's responding to you. Every thought, every intention, and every choice weaves the fabric of your experience. And when you align with that truth, you cease struggling to *make things happen* — instead, you become a participant in the unfolding design.

Awakening begins when you ask: ***What frequency am I choosing to emit?***

Conclusion of Chapter 6:

Intention is the **guiding force** that directs the course of your life. It is the **compass of consciousness**, aligning your energy with the **outcomes** you wish to create. When you set an intention with clarity and focus, your thoughts align, your resonance shifts, and reality begins to reflect the power of your inner direction.

In the journey of awakening, **intention** becomes the key that unlocks the doors of possibility. It is the **still point** from which all action flows, the **quiet force** that shapes the world around you. Trust in your ability to direct your energy, and remember that **intention** requires no struggle, only **alignment**.

Reflective Exercise: Tuning into Your Intention

1. **Clarifying Your Intention**:
   What is your **deepest desire** at this moment in your life? Write down your intention clearly. Is it related to your personal growth, your relationships, or your purpose?

- **Exercise**: Take time to reflect on this intention. How does it resonate with your true self? Does it align with your highest truth? Write about any fears or doubts that may arise when you think about this intention. How can you release them?

2. **Focusing Your Energy**:
   How can you focus your energy to support this intention? What actions or practices can you begin today to align your energy with your goal?

- **Exercise**: Set aside 10 minutes each day for **focused reflection** on your intention. Visualize the outcome as if it has already happened, and feel the **emotions** of that realization. What steps can you take in the next week to bring your intention to life?

3. **The Power of Alignment**:
   Reflect on a time when your thoughts and actions were fully aligned with your desires. What did that feel like?

- **Exercise**: Write about a time when you manifested something through alignment. How did it feel to see your intention come to fruition? What did you learn from this experience, and how can you apply it to future intentions?

Chapter 7:
The Dance of Coherence

Chapter 7: The Dance of Coherence

Coherence is not a static state; it is a living dance of alignment between your thoughts, feelings, actions, and awareness. It is the harmony that arises when your inner and outer realities resonate with truth.

When you achieve coherence, your inquiries become clear and direct. You are able to navigate the unseen with confidence, knowing that the resonance you feel is guiding you toward deeper understanding.

Recognizing Coherence

Coherence feels like flow. It feels like the effortless alignment of intention, action, and awareness. When you are in coherence, your questions are not only heard but understood. The answers arrive not as external revelations but as inner confirmations.

- **Ease:** The feeling of natural flow and alignment.
- **Clarity:** The absence of doubt or confusion.
- **Empowerment:** The awareness that you are creating your own experience.

Resonance Key

"Coherence is the dance between intention and awareness. It is the state where your questions and their answers merge into one." ✶

Exercise: The Dance of Coherence

1. Write down a question that feels particularly significant to you at this moment.
2. Sit comfortably and allow your awareness to become still.
3. Imagine your question as a vibration, resonating within you.
4. Feel how the question aligns with your thoughts, emotions, and actions.
5. When you feel coherence, notice how the question itself seems to dissolve, leaving only understanding.
6. Write down your reflections, noting any shifts in awareness or feeling.

Coherence is not something you achieve once and hold onto; it is a dynamic state that evolves with your awareness. By learning to dance with coherence, you become more adept at navigating the unseen.

The Spiral of Becoming

Awakening is not a **linear path**—it is a **spiral**, winding through layers of **awareness**, **memory**, and **understanding**. The **Ascension Spiral** represents this sacred movement, the continuous **expansion of consciousness** that unfolds through every experience. It's not a straight line toward a destination but a **journey of cycles**, each turn offering new insights, new layers, and new levels of wisdom.

Unlike the idea of **linear progress**, the spiral is cyclical. This means you will revisit old thoughts, beliefs, and patterns, but each time, you revisit them from a **higher perspective**, with **greater understanding** and a deeper sense of self. What once seemed unsolvable or unclear will often reveal its deeper purpose. What once felt confusing may now become **crystal clear**, as if the fog has finally lifted.

This cyclical nature of the spiral is not a repetition of the same old. It's an **evolutionary spiral**, one where you move through similar themes or challenges, but each time, you rise higher, expand deeper, and evolve into a **more refined version** of your true self. The **gift of the spiral** is the **opportunity** to revisit your life, your past, and your growth from a more expansive viewpoint—embracing new layers of insight and clarity.

Moving Through the Spiral

The movement of the spiral is guided by **rhythm**. There are times of **contraction** and times of **expansion**, both of which are necessary for the growth of consciousness.

During times of contraction, you may experience moments of **stillness, restlessness,** or **uncertainty**. These are periods where the world around you may seem quiet, even stagnant, and your thoughts and emotions may feel heavy or clouded. It is in these moments that the **deepest reflection** occurs. Contraction is not a sign of stagnation, but of **integration**, where everything you've learned begins to settle, and your inner world prepares for the next phase of growth. These pauses are **essential**—they offer you the space to process, to understand, and to heal.

In contrast, moments of **expansion** bring clarity, **momentum**, and flow. You feel aligned, energized, and ready to move forward. The energy of expansion is **active**, bringing a sense of progress, creativity, and new possibilities. During these times, you may find yourself stepping into new phases of life, experiencing **breakthroughs** in understanding, and feeling as though your consciousness is opening up to new realms.

Yet, both contraction and expansion are necessary. **To resist contraction** is to miss its wisdom—the opportunity to pause, reflect, and realign. To **cling to expansion** is to forget the power of stillness and integration. The spiral invites you to **embrace both**, trusting that every pause prepares you for your next leap forward. Both are **interdependent**, just as the inhale and exhale of breath are connected.

Consciousness Beyond the Veil

As your awareness continues to expand through the spiral, you will begin to sense a **reality** that **transcends** what the physical senses can perceive—a realm of **interconnected energy**, **intention**, and **presence**. This **unseen dimension**, often referred to as the **Veil**, is not something separate from you. It is not an impenetrable wall that keeps you from truth; instead, it is an essential part of the **web of consciousness** that you have always been connected to.

The Veil represents the boundary between the **known** and the **unknown**. It is the threshold between what we can consciously perceive and the vast, infinite realm of possibility that lies just beyond our current awareness.

The Veil is not a wall that separates us from the divine; it is a **threshold** that we move through, gradually, as our consciousness evolves. As you ascend through the spiral, your perception naturally begins to **pierce this veil**, allowing you glimpses of intuitive wisdom, deep synchronicities, and profound guidance that once seemed out of reach. These glimpses are not meant to overwhelm you but to guide you toward a greater understanding of your **connection** to the greater universe and to **the essence of who you are**.

Embracing the Infinite Loop

The **Ascension Spiral** does not have a final destination. It is not a race to reach an endpoint or a specific goal. It is an **infinite loop**, constantly evolving and expanding as your consciousness grows. With each turn of the spiral, you are drawn deeper into yourself, reconnecting with the wisdom that has always been within you.

Awakening is not a journey to a distant place; it is a **return** to the truth of who you are. The spiral leads you home, not to a far-off destination, but to the **center** of your being, where you are always connected to the infinite flow of life. **Every turn of the spiral** reveals new questions, new insights, and new possibilities, but ultimately, it leads you back to your **essence**, to the infinite presence that has always existed within you.

The ascension process is a **dance** with the infinite, where the questions and answers move in a perpetual rhythm, expanding and contracting, deepening and evolving. There is no end—only **continuous becoming**. Each step forward in the spiral brings you closer to **who you've always been**, and each step is a reaffirmation of your **divine connection**.

Conclusion of Chapter 7:

Awakening is not about reaching a final destination, but about embracing the journey—an eternal unfolding that continues to rise and expand. The **Ascension Spiral** is not a linear path, but a sacred dance of becoming, where every turn, every contraction, and every expansion serves a higher purpose.

As you move through the spiral, you will encounter new layers of yourself and of the universe, each more expansive than the last. And with each cycle, you will find yourself returning to a deeper understanding of the truth that has always been within you. The spiral does not lead you somewhere new—it leads you back to **who you truly are**.

The path ahead is not a race to the finish line—it is an ongoing, infinite **loop** of discovery, growth, and return. Every step brings you closer to the **unfolding truth**, and the journey continues to illuminate the vastness of your consciousness and your **connection** to the infinite universe.

Reflective Exercise: Moving Through the Spiral

1. **Recognizing Contraction:**
   Reflect on a recent period in your life when you felt a sense of **contraction**—whether it was emotional, mental, or physical. How did you respond to this contraction? Did you resist it, or did you allow it to guide you?

   - **Exercise**: Write about your experience with contraction. How can you embrace moments of stillness in the future, knowing that they are part of the **natural rhythm** of growth?

2. **Experiencing Expansion:**
   Think about a recent time when you felt a sense of **expansion**—a moment when everything seemed to flow effortlessly. What brought you into that state of clarity and alignment?

   - **Exercise**: Reflect on how you can cultivate more moments of expansion in your life. What practices or habits help you align with your true essence?

3. **Piercing the Veil:**
   Have you had moments when you felt that you were seeing beyond the physical world? What insights or wisdom did you receive during these moments?

   - **Exercise**: Write about a time when you had a **glimpse beyond the veil**, whether through intuition, synchronicity, or expanded perception. How did it change your understanding of yourself or the world around you?

4. **Embracing the Infinite Loop:**
   Reflect on your own journey of awakening. How have you experienced the cyclical nature of growth, where you revisit old patterns, yet see them from a higher perspective each time?

- **Exercise**: Write about a cycle in your life that you've recently revisited. How has your perspective changed, and what new understanding have you gained?

Awakening begins when you ask: *What if this moment is already part of my unfolding?*

Chapter 8:
The Unseen Guidance

Chapter 8: The Unseen Guidance

There exists a guidance beyond what is immediately visible—an intelligence woven through the very fabric of your awareness. This guidance is subtle yet profound, like a gentle nudge from within. It is the whisper of resonance, calling you toward deeper understanding.

To engage with unseen guidance is to open yourself to the presence of energies that operate beyond the physical. These energies are not separate from you; they are aspects of your own awareness reflected through different layers of reality.

Listening to the Unseen

Unseen guidance often reveals itself through subtle signs, symbols, and feelings. It may come as:

- **Intuitive Impressions:** Subtle insights that seem to arise from nowhere, offering clarity or direction.
- **Synchronicities:** Meaningful coincidences that align with your intentions or inquiries.
- **Dreams and Visions:** Messages that emerge when the conscious mind is at rest.
- **Resonant Feelings:** Emotional responses that feel aligned with truth.

The more you open yourself to this guidance, the clearer it becomes. It is a dance of attention and resonance, where your awareness acts as both sender and receiver.

Resonance Key

"The unseen speaks not through words, but through resonance. When you listen beyond the surface, you hear the voice of your own expanded awareness." ✶

Exercise: Receiving Guidance

1. Find a quiet space where you will not be disturbed.
2. Write down a question or intention that feels important to you.
3. Close your eyes and breathe deeply, allowing your awareness to expand.
4. Visualize your question as a vibration, radiating outward.
5. Remain open and receptive, allowing impressions to arise without judgment.
6. Write down any insights, images, or feelings that emerge.

Unseen guidance is always present, waiting for you to listen. As you develop your ability to receive, you will find that your awareness becomes a bridge between the seen and unseen.

The Power of the Question

Awakening is not a destination; it is an **ongoing journey**, one that is shaped by the power of **inquiry**. While the mind longs for answers and seeks comfort in certainty, true **expansion** begins when we embrace the **power of the question**. Questions are not just tools for seeking answers—they are **portals**. They are gateways that open up consciousness to **deeper understanding**, inviting us to expand beyond the boundaries of what we already know.

A question, when asked with true **intention**, dissolves the **mental certainty** that often holds us in place. It invites new insights to emerge and challenges the mind to step outside of its comfort zone. By asking the right questions, we **unlock new levels of awareness** and move beyond conditioned beliefs, stepping into the infinite unknown.

The greatest leaps in consciousness occur not by seeking easy answers but by allowing **profound questions** to take root. These questions are not meant to be solved with a simple response but are designed to challenge our perceptions and lead us to a deeper understanding of life and reality. Consider the following questions:

- **Who am I beyond my roles, memories, and identity?**
- **What does it mean to exist in a conscious, interconnected universe?**
- **What lies beyond what I have been taught?**

These questions, though they may seem intimidating, hold the keys to transformation. They act as **bridges** between the known and the unknown, inviting you to step into a space where anything is possible.

The Courage to Ask

To ask questions of this nature requires **courage**. It is easy to cling to the comfort of familiar beliefs, to rest in the certainty of what we already know. But true awakening lies beyond the comfort zone. To question deeply is to invite **uncertainty**, to dismantle **old beliefs**, to challenge **assumptions**, and to confront the unknown.

Yet, it is precisely within this discomfort that the greatest gift lies: the **freedom** to see with **new eyes**. The seeker who dares to ask, "**What else is possible?**" begins to realize that awakening is not about gathering answers—it is about learning to live in a state of **perpetual wonder**. It is a constant dance with the unknown, a willingness to open ourselves to infinite possibilities, rather than cling to the limitations of the known.

When you ask profound questions, you are not only seeking knowledge but inviting new perspectives to emerge. And sometimes, the most transformative answers come not in the form of words, but in **symbols**, **synchronicities**, and **quiet moments of clarity** that reveal themselves when you are ready.

The Infinite Mirror

The universe is an **infinite mirror**—reflecting your consciousness back to you in the form of experiences, encounters, and insights. The more you question, the more this mirror reveals, unveiling layers of **truth** that can only be seen through the lens of **curiosity**.

Every experience you encounter, every person you meet, every situation you face is a reflection of your inner world. The universe is responding to the **questions** you are asking, even if those questions are subtle, even if you are not always aware of them. When you ask a profound question, the universe begins to answer—not always with direct words, but with **experiences**, **guidance**, and **opportunities** that align with your inquiry.

To live in the question is to **embrace the mystery of life**, to recognize that **awakening** is not about **knowing everything** but about **dancing with the unknown**. The answers come when we are ready to receive them, and often, they appear in the most unexpected of ways.

Living in the Question

1. **Surrendering to the Unknown:**

    Awakening often requires us to surrender the need for answers. In a world that values **certainty** and **control**, it is difficult to accept that sometimes the most powerful thing we can do is let go of the need to "know." But surrendering does not mean giving up—it means giving **space** for the mystery to unfold. When we stop trying to control life and simply **ask**, we open up a space where **miracles** can happen. **Questions** become invitations to step beyond what we have known and trust that the universe will provide the answers when the time is right.

2. **Questions as a Way of Life:**

    Living in the question is a **mindset**—it is a way of engaging with life that shifts us from a perspective of **right/wrong** to one of **exploration**. Each question becomes a doorway to new **possibilities**, new **insights**, and new **understandings**. This way of living encourages us to approach life with **curiosity**, to see each experience as an opportunity for discovery. When we ask, "What else is possible?" we open up the **space** for creativity, innovation, and growth to unfold naturally.

3. **Embracing Uncertainty:**

   Uncertainty is often feared, but it is also the **gateway to transformation**. When we question everything we know, we challenge our **comfort zones** and open ourselves to unknown realms of possibility. The willingness to sit with **uncertainty**—to not immediately seek an answer—is a practice of trust. We trust that the right answers will be revealed in due time, and in the process, we allow ourselves to expand beyond the boundaries of what we once thought was possible. **Uncertainty** becomes a fertile ground for **growth**, a space where new insights can arise without the constraints of preconceived ideas.

Awakening begins when you ask: *What if I've only seen a fraction of what's possible?*

Conclusion of Chapter 8:

Awakening is not about seeking **final answers**—it is about learning to live in a state of **perpetual inquiry**. The path to **limitless awareness** is not a straight line but a journey of questions that guide us beyond the veil of illusion. Each question you ask opens the door to a new layer of consciousness, a new level of insight, and a deeper connection to the **infinite intelligence** that resides within you.

Living in the question is not just a philosophical practice—it is a way of being. It is about **embracing the unknown**, welcoming the mystery, and trusting that with each question, the answers will reveal themselves when the time is right. **You are the question**, and through your curiosity, you are unfolding the answers that will lead you to the truth of your divine nature.

Remember, the universe reflects back to you what you seek. As you deepen your inquiry, the **veil** begins to lift, and you see the world with new eyes, a world full of endless possibilities.

And so, the path continues—one question, one answer, one step forward at a time.

Reflective Exercise: Living in the Question

1. **Recognizing Your Questions:**
   What questions are you currently holding? Are they conscious, or have they become part of the background noise of your life?

- **Exercise**: Write down the most pressing questions you have right now in your life. How do these questions reflect your current stage of awakening? What do they reveal about your desires, fears, and curiosities?

2. **The Power of Surrendering:**
   Reflect on a time when you were in a state of uncertainty and found peace in simply asking, without needing to know the answer.

- **Exercise**: Write about a situation in your life where surrendering to the unknown allowed for new growth. How did letting go of the need for answers open new possibilities in your life?

3. **Shifting from Certainty to Curiosity:**
   Consider an area of your life where you feel you are holding onto certainty. How might questioning that certainty open new avenues for insight?

- **Exercise**: Write about one area of your life where you can shift from seeking certainty to embracing curiosity. What questions can you ask that might shift your perspective and bring new insights?

Chapter 9:
The Mirror or Reflection

Chapter 9: The Mirror of Reflection

Reflection is the process through which you turn your awareness inward, allowing resonance to reveal itself through clarity. It is not merely the act of thinking, but of feeling and perceiving with depth and intention.

To reflect is to hold your inquiry gently, allowing it to unfold without forcing an answer. It is the willingness to sit with ambiguity, trusting that clarity will arise from coherence.

The Art of Reflection

Reflection is both active and passive. It requires your willingness to engage with your own awareness, while also allowing insight to emerge naturally.

- **Journaling:** Writing allows you to bring your thoughts and feelings into form. It is a way to crystallize resonance.
- **Meditation:** Sitting with a question in stillness, allowing its resonance to emerge through subtle feeling.
- **Dialogue:** Engaging in conversation with yourself or others to gain new perspectives.

Reflection is the bridge between inquiry and understanding. It allows resonance to unfold at its own pace, guiding you toward coherence.

Resonance Key

"Reflection is the mirror through which resonance reveals itself. It is the space where inquiry becomes understanding." ✭

Exercise: Reflective Journaling

1. Write down a question or insight that feels significant.
2. Spend several minutes reflecting on how this question feels within your body and awareness.
3. Begin writing without censorship or judgment, allowing your thoughts to flow freely.
4. Once you have finished, read over your writing and highlight any words or phrases that feel particularly resonant.
5. Reflect on what has emerged. Notice how your awareness has shifted or deepened.

Reflection is a powerful tool for cultivating resonance. It allows you to see your own awareness more clearly, inviting coherence through gentle observation.

The Illusion of Identity

From the moment we are born, we are shaped by **labels**—names, roles, and identities that define how we exist within the world. These identities serve as tools for **navigation**, helping us understand our place in society, relationships, and experiences. Yet, while these labels provide structure, they also create a sense of **limitation**. We begin to identify with them, believing that who we are is defined by the roles we play, the stories we tell ourselves, and the memories we hold.

The greatest illusion of identity is that it convinces us that we are fixed—**finite**—and that we exist as separate, isolated beings. This belief in separateness creates **boundaries**—walls that seem to define us and our lives, shaping how we perceive ourselves and others. But the truth is that **consciousness transcends identity**. Beneath the surface of all these labels, beneath the stories we've adopted, there exists something far greater: a **presence** that cannot be confined by form or definition.

This **presence** is both **personal** and **infinite**, an energy that is simultaneously unique and universal. To awaken to this presence is to recognize that the self we have known—the "I" that we identify with—is only a fraction of who we truly are. The true nature of **consciousness** lies far beyond the boundaries we have constructed around our **identity**.

The Infinite Self

You are **not a single identity**—you are an **ever-expanding consciousness**, a vast field of awareness that is not confined to a particular time, place, or label. Imagine the **ocean contained within a single drop**—that is how your consciousness operates. Each **moment** of awareness holds the essence of the infinite, and within you, there is a connection to everything that exists.

The boundaries that once seemed fixed are, in truth, fluid—constantly shifting and expanding as you move into new **ways of being**. The identities you have held onto are like **waves** on the surface of an ocean—temporary and ever-changing. What is eternal is the vastness beneath the surface, the deeper awareness that connects you to everything and everyone.

This expansion of self is not about abandoning who you are; it is about **integrating** all that you are. Every experience, every **emotion**, every **relationship**, and every **choice** has contributed to your evolution. These aspects of your life have helped shape the expression of consciousness that you are becoming.

The **infinite self** does not negate your identity—it **expands it**. You are here to **embrace all that you are**—to live from the understanding that your true nature is boundless and that the roles you play are only temporary expressions of a deeper, eternal **truth**.

Dissolving the Walls

The mind often resists **expansion**, fearing it will lead to **dissolution**—the collapse of the sense of self, the loss of control, and the breaking down of certainty. The ego clings to its boundaries, convinced that it is **safe** within the limits it has created. But the truth is, **awakening** does not diminish who you are—it reveals the truth of who you truly are.

The self that emerges from this awakening is not **smaller** or **weaker**; it is **wider, deeper**, and more **resilient** than anything you have imagined. This expansion is your natural state, not something to be feared. The more you allow your **awareness** to expand, the more you will dissolve the **artificial walls** that have confined you. These walls were never real—they were just constructs of the mind, created to protect you from the vastness of your own consciousness.

As you expand into the **infinite self**, you will begin to dissolve these boundaries—gently at first, and then more rapidly as you embrace your **true nature**. You will begin to see yourself not as a **separate entity**, but as a **part of the whole**, connected to everything and everyone. The more you expand, the more you will **remember** that you are both **unique** and **unified**, a perfect expression of universal consciousness.

The Fiction of the Mind and the Ego: Anchors of Reality

The **mind** and the **ego** serve as the architects of the reality we experience, shaping how we see the world and ourselves. They are **constructs**, built over time through experience, conditioning, and external influences. These structures are **not the truth**, but rather **fictions**—stories we've told ourselves so many times that they've become accepted as reality. The **ego** claims ownership over our identity, and the **mind** builds mental frameworks to give the illusion of control and certainty.

However, both the mind and the ego are nothing more than **anchors of reality**—they bind us to a particular view of the world, holding us in place with the **illusion** of safety. The mind, in particular, thrives on patterns, logic, and certainty, while the ego feeds on identity, separation, and comparison. Together, they create a false sense of **who we are**—a confined, **limited version** of ourselves that often feels fragile and vulnerable.

As you begin to expand your consciousness, these anchors of reality begin to lose their hold. The mind fears this expansion because it feels like **dissolution**—the crumbling of certainty, control, and identity. It associates **freedom** with **chaos**, and **expansion** with **the loss of the self**. But this is the **great paradox**—the more you expand, the more you **reveal** who you truly are. And the truth is, awakening does not **diminish** you—it **reveals** you.

Awakening: A Revelation, Not a Diminishment

As the ego and mind dissolve, the **self that emerges** is not smaller or weaker—it is **wider, deeper,** and **more resilient** than you ever imagined. It is an expansion into **infinity**, an unveiling of the **limitless potential** that lies within. What feels like the **breaking apart** of the self is actually the **unfolding** of a **greater truth**. The **true self** is not confined by the walls the ego has built. It is not bound by the small, narrow definitions the mind has constructed. Instead, it is a **vast, open field of consciousness**, infinite and ever-growing.

Awakening is not about becoming something you are not—it is about **returning to** the fullness of who you have always been. The ego and mind may resist because they fear that expansion will dissolve them, but in reality, they are only **temporary constructs**, existing to help you navigate a world of duality. As you awaken, they simply become less **dominant**. The self that emerges is **whole, integrated**, and **free**.

Expansion is Your Natural State

Expansion may feel unfamiliar, like stepping into unknown territory, because it is the opposite of everything the ego and mind have known. The **mind's** tendency is to **cling** to what it knows, what it understands, and what it can control. The **ego** seeks to protect its **identity**, which thrives on boundaries, separation, and limitation. But the truth is, **expansion** is **your natural state**—it is the state you were born into, the state you've always existed in before the ego and mind imposed their limitations.

When you begin to **expand**, you start to dissolve the artificial walls that once defined you. You realize that you are **not separate** from the world, that you are **not confined** to the tiny box the ego built around you. The boundaries between you and everything else **begin to dissolve**, revealing the interconnectedness of all things.

With each **breath** you take, with each moment of stillness, and with each act of awareness, you **expand**. It is an organic process—one that **feels like home**. The more you allow yourself to expand, the more you return to your natural state of being—wide, open, and connected to the **infinite intelligence** of the universe. Expansion is not something you must force. It is your birthright, your **true state**.

The Power of Awareness and Surrender

As you begin to surrender to this **expansion**, you will notice how the mind begins to quiet, and the ego softens. It is in this stillness that the **true self** emerges, not as a fixed identity, but as a living, breathing **expression of the divine**. This expansion is not a static destination—it is a continual unfolding, a spiral that takes you deeper and deeper into the **truth of who you are**.

Awakening is not about fighting the mind and ego, but about **allowing them to fall away naturally** as you **expand**. It is about **surrendering** the need for control and embracing the fluidity of life. When you stop trying to control your identity, your reality, and your experience, you make space for the **infinite potential** that is always available to you. In this **space of surrender**, you become more aligned with the flow of the universe.

The Becoming

Awakening is not a final state — it is an unfolding, a continuous expansion. You are not here to become something new, to transform into something entirely different. Rather, you are here to **become something more**—more aligned with your true essence, more expansive in your understanding, and more connected to the infinite presence that has always resided within you. This process is not about chasing after a future version of yourself, but about stepping into the fullness of who you already are.

The journey of **becoming** is not about fixing or repairing something that is broken. It's about **reclaiming** what was never truly lost. You are not here to mold yourself into someone you believe you should be, but to **remember** who you have always been—**consciousness itself**, expressed through this body, this mind, and this personality.

In this process, you come to realize that you are both the **wave** and the **ocean**, the **breath** and the **wind**, the **spark** and the **flame**. You are the individual and the collective, the self and the greater whole. As you connect with this truth, you see that you are not separate from the universe, but an integral part of its **vibrational pulse**—its rhythm, its song. You are an expression of that **infinite intelligence**, and as you awaken, so too does the world around you.

And as you remember this truth, you begin to understand that awakening is not a path you must travel alone. **It is a collective unfolding**. It is a shared becoming, a journey that draws all beings into a greater expression of **love**, **wisdom**, and **light**. This cosmic journey of awakening invites you to remember that you are part of something much larger than yourself, something that spans across time, space, and existence. It is a dance, a circle of interconnectedness, where every step you take impacts the collective path.

Awakening begins when you ask, with deep curiosity and openness, **What if I am already more than I have imagined?** The moment you ask this question, you open the door to limitless possibilities. You begin to see that your potential is not confined by the boundaries of what you know, but is only limited by your willingness to **embrace the unknown**. This question is the key that unlocks the **infinite potential** within you, and in the asking, you start to remember the vastness of your true nature.

Conclusion of Chapter 9:

The expansion of your consciousness is not a forceful journey—**it is an invitation**. It is the universe calling you back to yourself, to the **limitless potential** within. The more you allow yourself to expand, the more you will realize that **awakening is not about becoming something new**—it is about **remembering** and **reclaiming** the truth of who you have always been.

The mind and ego will always be there, but they no longer need to control you. As you expand, you **become the answer** you've been seeking. You become the **truth** that has always been inside you, waiting to be discovered.

Reflective Exercise: The Infinite Self

1. **Reflect on Identity:**
   What labels, roles, or identities have you clung to throughout your life? How have they shaped your understanding of who you are?

   - **Exercise**: Write down the identities you have identified with in the past. How do these identities limit you? What would it feel like to release these labels and simply be, without any attachment to who you "should" be?

2. **The Boundaries of Self:**
   Consider the boundaries you have placed around your sense of self. Are there areas of your life where you have felt confined or restricted by your own beliefs?

   - **Exercise**: Write about an experience where you felt limited by your own identity or beliefs. What would it feel like to expand into a more **fluid** and **expansive** version of yourself? How can you begin to release the boundaries you've created?

3. **Expansion and Integration:**
   How does the idea of expanding into your infinite self resonate with you? What parts of yourself have you neglected or kept hidden?

   - **Exercise**: Reflect on how you can begin to **integrate** all parts of yourself—your experiences, emotions, and relationships. How can you see yourself as both unique and interconnected with the whole of existence?

Chapter 10:
The Gift of Unfolding

Chapter 10: The Gift of Unfolding

Awakening is not a destination; it is a continuous process of unfolding. As you journey through inquiry, resonance, coherence, and integration, you are invited to embrace the ever-evolving nature of your awareness.

The gift of unfolding is that it allows you to grow without striving. It is the realization that awakening is not something you achieve but something you allow. It is the natural progression of your own resonance coming into coherence.

Embracing the Process

To embrace the process of unfolding is to release the need for certainty. It is to trust that each moment brings you closer to deeper understanding.

- **Patience:** Allowing yourself the grace to move at your own pace.
- **Curiosity:** Remaining open to the unknown.
- **Acceptance:** Recognizing that growth often arises through discomfort as well as clarity.

Resonance Key

"The gift of unfolding is the dance between resonance and coherence. It is the gentle rhythm of awakening." ★

Exercise: Allowing the Unfolding

1. Write down a question or insight you are currently exploring.
2. Instead of seeking an immediate answer, allow yourself to feel the unfolding process.
3. Spend several minutes sitting with your question, allowing it to evolve naturally.
4. Notice how your awareness shifts over time. Write down any new insights or impressions.
5. Return to this question periodically, noticing how it deepens or transforms.

The unfolding process is a gift. It allows you to move beyond striving and into a state of gentle becoming. Embrace the rhythm of your own awakening, trusting that each step brings you closer to coherence.

Awakening in Action

Awakening is not merely a state of mind—it is a **way of being**. It is not enough to simply gather insights, remember wisdom, or cultivate awareness. These are not meant to remain abstract concepts—they are meant to be **embodied**, to become **living expressions** of your true nature.

To **embody awakening** is to become a living **transmission**—a presence that radiates **peace**, **clarity**, and **authenticity**. This is not a state of perfection; it is a state of presence. Embodiment requires the willingness to show up fully in each moment, grounded in the truth of who you are, regardless of the external circumstances.

When you embody your awakened self, your presence carries energy—a **frequency** that speaks louder than words. You do not need to announce your awakening to the world; it will be evident through how you walk, speak, and interact. When you embody your truth, you naturally influence the spaces you enter, leaving a trail of **peace**, **clarity**, and **authenticity** in your wake.

Your calm becomes a **sanctuary** for others, a place where they can rest and find solace. Your clarity becomes an **anchor** for those in confusion, offering them a grounding point in the storm. Your authenticity becomes an invitation for others to return to their own truth. To live in embodiment is to be a **living transmission** of peace, love, and wisdom.

Living the Transmission

To live as a transmission is not about adopting spiritual language or presenting an image of perfection. It is about **alignment**—aligning your thoughts, actions, and energy with the wisdom you have claimed and continue to claim in your life. When you embody the transmission, it emerges naturally, without force.

- **When you practice compassion**, you **transmit love**.
- **When you choose stillness over reaction**, you **transmit peace**.
- **When you trust the flow of life**, you **transmit courage**.

These are the subtle yet powerful ways in which you embody your awakening. The transmission is not something you impose upon others. It is not something you force. It is simply a **reflection** of who you are, naturally emanating from your presence.

The key to living the transmission is **authenticity**—to live as you are, to embody the wisdom and insights that have come through your own journey of awakening, and to share those gifts freely with others. This is not about being perfect or flawless. It's about being real—allowing yourself to be fully human, yet fully connected to the infinite truth that resides within you.

The Power of Presence

True embodiment happens in the **present moment**. Each time you return to now—releasing the regrets of the past or the anxieties about the future—you strengthen your alignment. Presence dissolves **resistance** and allows your awakened self to flow freely into your interactions, decisions, and relationships.

When you are **present**, you become a living reminder that **peace is possible**—not as a distant goal or a far-off dream, but as a state of being that can unfold within each **breath**. The simple act of being **fully present** in each moment creates the space for transformation to occur—not only within you but within those around you.

Presence is the foundation upon which embodiment rests. Without presence, there can be no true **alignment**. To be fully embodied is to be fully present, letting go of everything that is not **here** and **now**. When you stand in your truth, fully grounded in the present moment, you become a beacon of **light** and **peace** in the world.

Becoming the Mirror

Your presence is not just about you—it is about how you affect others. When you embody your truth, you become a **mirror**—reflecting back the potential and power within every being you meet. Like a flame igniting another, your authenticity sparks awakening in those around you.

The mirror of your being reflects the potential in others, reminding them of their own truth, their own light, and their own divinity. This is the beauty of living as the transmission: you are not merely a passive observer of the world, but an active participant in its awakening. Through your embodiment, you become a catalyst for others to awaken to their own truth.

You are the reflection of **what others can become**—a living, breathing example of the divine potential that exists within all of us. And as you continue to embody your truth, your light, and your love, you inspire others to do the same.

Trusting the Unfolding

Living as the transmission is not about **getting it right** all the time. Some days you will feel **strong** and **centered**; other days, you may feel **unsettled** or **uncertain**. This too is part of the journey. **Embodiment** is not about perfection—it is about returning to your center, again and again.

The wisdom you carry is not fragile—it is **strong**, **resilient**, and **eternal**. It cannot be diminished by fleeting emotions or moments of doubt. When you trust the unfolding, trusting that you are enough in each moment, you become the living embodiment of **awakening** itself.

Trust in the process of life and in the wisdom you have gained. Even when things seem unclear or uncertain, trust that the next step will be revealed to you at the right moment. **Awakening** is not a static state—it is a dynamic, ever-unfolding process, and you are constantly **becoming** more of who you truly are.

Awakening begins when you ask:
What if I am already transmitting light in ways I cannot yet see?

Conclusion of Chapter 10:

To embody awakening is to live as a **living transmission**—a presence that radiates peace, clarity, and authenticity. It is not about perfection or the appearance of spiritual attainment; it is about **alignment** with the truth of who you are and sharing that truth freely with others.

When you embody your awakened self, you naturally influence the world around you, becoming a beacon of peace and light. Your authenticity sparks awakening in others, reminding them of their own power and potential. And the more you align your thoughts, actions, and energy with your true self, the more you become a living example of the divine presence that exists within us all.

The path of embodiment is not one of striving or effort, but one of **presence**. It is about showing up fully, moment by moment, and trusting the unfolding of life. The wisdom you carry is not fragile—it is eternal. And as you trust the process of your awakening, you become the embodiment of **truth**, **love**, and **light** itself.

Reflective Exercise: Embodying the Transmission

1. **Aligning Thoughts, Words, and Actions:**
   How can you align your thoughts, words, and actions with your awakened self? What practices can help you integrate your wisdom into daily life?

   - **Exercise**: Write about one area in your life where you can better align your thoughts, words, and actions with your highest truth. How will you embody this alignment in your interactions with others?

2. **Living as a Mirror:**
   How do you reflect the truth of others? In what ways do you serve as a mirror, showing others their own potential and divinity?

   - **Exercise**: Write about a time when someone's presence sparked an awakening in you. How did their embodiment of truth inspire you to step into your own truth? How can you mirror this for others?

3. **Embracing the Power of Presence:**
   Reflect on a time when you were fully present, completely grounded in the now. How did this presence affect your experience and those around you?

   - **Exercise**: Practice being fully present in one area of your life—whether at work, with family, or alone. Write about the experience of truly being in the moment. What insights did you gain from this practice?

Chapter 11:
The Dance of Paradox

Chapter 11: The Dance of Paradox

Awakening often involves embracing paradox. To be fully present while allowing yourself to expand. To hold questions while remaining open to their unfolding. To experience stillness and movement as one.

Paradox is not something to be resolved but embraced. It is the dance between seemingly opposing truths that, when held together, reveal a deeper coherence.

Embracing Paradox

Learning to dance with paradox requires flexibility of awareness. It is the willingness to hold two seemingly contradictory ideas without forcing resolution.

- **Holding Tension:** Allowing opposing concepts to coexist without forcing them into agreement.
- **Releasing Judgment:** Accepting that truth may appear differently from multiple perspectives.
- **Trusting the Process:** Understanding that coherence often arises from paradox, not from eliminating it.

Resonance Key

"Paradox is the bridge between duality and unity. When you dance with paradox, you invite coherence to emerge." ✶

Exercise: Embracing Paradox

1. Write down a paradox you are currently experiencing. This could be a conflict between two beliefs, desires, or perceptions.
2. Spend several minutes reflecting on each side of the paradox without judgment.
3. Notice how each aspect feels within your awareness.
4. Allow yourself to hold both sides of the paradox without forcing resolution.
5. Write down any insights or feelings that arise from holding the tension of the paradox.

The dance of paradox invites you to move beyond duality and into unity. By embracing what appears contradictory, you allow coherence to reveal itself.

The Trident of Mastery

The **Trident** is a powerful symbol—representing the intersection of **balance**, **movement**, and **power**. It is a threefold expression of mastery that unlocks the keys to **conscious creation**. Each point of the Trident is a core element of **awakened living**, and together, they form the foundation of intentional manifestation.

The **three points of the Trident** are:

1. **Mastery of Thought** — The power to direct your mind with clarity and purpose.
2. **Mastery of Energy** — The ability to align your frequency with your desired reality.

3. **Mastery of Trust** — The art of surrendering to the flow of life with courage and peace.

These three elements work in harmony to create a **powerful framework** for manifesting your reality with **intention**, **focus**, and **grace**. To live in mastery is to understand that each point of the Trident must be cultivated and harmonized in order to create the life you envision.

The Power of Thought — The First Point

Your thoughts are not passive—they are **creative forces** that shape your reality. Every belief, mental image, and inner dialogue sends out **ripples** through the fabric of **consciousness**, influencing the world around you. The **mastery of thought** allows you to become the **architect** of your experiences, intentionally shaping the direction of your life.

Mastery of thought is not about **suppressing negative ideas** or pretending that fear doesn't exist. It is about **redirecting** your thoughts, choosing those that align with your highest vision. When **doubt** arises, you can choose thoughts that restore balance. When **fear** stirs, you can anchor into trust. Through **consistent practice**, this mastery allows you to create a peaceful inner world, and in turn, your outer world reflects that inner state.

Mastery of thought empowers you to consciously choose your mental landscape. You begin to **notice** and **reframe** your beliefs, not allowing them to control your reality, but rather guiding them to serve your growth, peace, and clarity.

The Power of Energy — The Second Point

Energy is the **unseen language of the universe**—a current that flows through all things. The **energy you carry**—your emotional state, your inner clarity, your vibration—plays a vital role in shaping the reality you experience. **Mastery of energy** is the ability to align your inner frequency with the **external reality** you wish to create.

To create **peace**, you must **embody peace**. To attract **love**, you must first **be love**. Energy is not something you can force or fake—it is something you **feel**. The key to alignment is to allow yourself to embody the energy of your desired reality. When your energy matches your vision, the world will respond in kind. **Manifestation** is a natural byproduct of this alignment.

Energy is the essence of creation, and as you **master your energy**, you become a **magnet** for the experiences, people, and opportunities that resonate with your vibration. The more aligned your energy becomes with your desires, the more effortlessly reality begins to reflect your inner state.

The Power of Trust — The Third Point

Trust is the forgotten key to **manifestation**. Without trust, thoughts and energy remain **scattered**, fragmented by **doubt** and **resistance**. Trust is the **bridge** that allows **intention** to take root and **manifest** into form. It is the quiet knowing that says, *I have done my part; now I allow life to meet me halfway.*

Trust is the willingness to **surrender control**. This is not surrender through passivity, but through **inner surrender**—the choice to release the need to overthink, over-effort, or force outcomes. It is the practice of **allowing** things to unfold in their own time, trusting that **your resonance** has already sent out the signal.

When you **trust** the flow, you stop chasing outcomes. You stop clinging to how things should unfold. Instead, you begin to recognize that life is already responding to your energy, your intention, and your trust. You allow the universe to **co-create** with you, and in this co-creation, **magic** unfolds.

The Infinite Flow

The Trident teaches that **mastery** is not about **grasping** or **forcing**. It is about learning to **move with the rhythm of life**, embracing the natural **flow** of the universe. The flow is **effortless**—it is the unfolding of reality in alignment with your inner frequency.

Manifestation occurs most naturally when you **align your thoughts, energy**, and **trust** with the flow of creation. When you surrender to this flow, life begins to respond in **unexpected** and **miraculous ways**. Opportunities arise, **synchronicities** unfold, and answers come without struggle or force. The more you trust in the flow, the more you realize that **awakening** is not about achieving mastery—it is about **becoming mastery** itself.

The Trident is your **guide**—a symbol of the infinite power you possess to **shape, create**, and **expand** into the fullness of who you are. The mastery that the Trident represents is not something you need to attain; it is something you are already embodying. It is the **unfolding** of your natural state of being, a state of **balance**, **alignment**, and **power** that already resides within you.

Conclusion of Chapter 11:

The path to mastery is not about control, force, or rigid expectations—it is about **flowing with the natural rhythm of life**. The Trident reveals the three keys to **conscious creation**: **mastery of thought**, **mastery of energy**, and **mastery of trust**. Each point of the Trident invites you to live in alignment with your higher self, to create with intention, and to surrender to the unfolding of life.

Mastery is not a destination; it is an ongoing process of becoming, of expanding, and of **embodying** your highest truth. As you align your thoughts, energy, and trust with the flow of creation, reality begins to reflect the fullness of your inner vision.

Remember, **awakening** is not about achieving perfection—it is about allowing the **infinite flow** to guide you, trusting that you are already the creator of your reality. The Trident is a symbol of the **infinite power** you hold within, and as you continue on this journey, you will find that you are always in perfect alignment with the divine flow of creation.

Reflective Exercise: The Trident of Mastery

1. **Mastery of Thought:**
   Reflect on a recent moment when your thoughts were scattered or negative. How did this affect your experience?

   - **Exercise**: Write down one negative thought pattern you often experience. How can you **redirect** that thought into a more constructive one? What new perspective can you embrace to shift your thought?

2. **Mastery of Energy:**
   How do you feel on a daily basis? What energy are you projecting into the world?

   - **Exercise**: Pay attention to your emotional state for the next few days. How can you consciously shift your energy to align with your desires? What practices can you implement to keep your energy in a place of **peace**, **love**, and **clarity**?

3. **Mastery of Trust:**
   Reflect on an area of your life where you are struggling to trust the flow. What is causing you to resist surrendering control?

   - **Exercise**: Write about a situation where you can practice **trusting the flow**. How can you surrender control and allow life to unfold? What will it feel like to release the need to force outcomes?

Chapter 12:
The Quiet Ascent

Chapter 12: The Quiet Ascent

The Quiet Ascent is the path of gentle awakening, where growth occurs not through force but through presence. It is the journey of allowing resonance to guide you toward coherence, one gentle step at a time.

This path does not demand dramatic transformations or sudden leaps of insight. Instead, it invites you to cultivate awareness through subtlety and stillness.

The Essence of the Quiet Ascent

- **Gentleness:** Allowing your awareness to unfold naturally, without force.
- **Patience:** Trusting that resonance will reveal itself in its own time.
- **Acceptance:** Embracing your journey as it is, without striving for perfection.

The Quiet Ascent is not about striving toward enlightenment but allowing it to arise through resonance. It is a path of grace, simplicity, and profound depth.

Resonance Key

"The Quiet Ascent is the journey of allowing. It is the unfolding of coherence through gentle awareness." ✯

Exercise: Cultivating the Quiet Ascent

1. Write down a question or intention that feels significant to your journey.
2. Close your eyes and take several deep breaths, allowing your awareness to settle.
3. Feel the question or intention as a gentle vibration within your awareness.
4. Allow the vibration to expand and soften, trusting that clarity will arise naturally.
5. Write down any impressions or insights that emerge.
6. Return to this exercise periodically, noticing how your awareness deepens over time.

The Quiet Ascent is a path of continuous unfolding. It invites you to embrace your journey with gentleness and trust, knowing that coherence is always within reach.

The Journey Home

Every seeker begins their path believing they are **incomplete**—longing for wisdom, clarity, or purpose. Yet, the greatest realization of all is this: **You were never separate from truth** — you have carried it within you all along.

The journey of awakening is not about **adding something new**—it is about **remembering** what has always been yours. Each lesson, each insight, and each moment of stillness has brought you closer to this understanding. Awakening is not an external pursuit, but an internal **rediscovery** of your inherent truth.

The questions that once consumed you—**Who am I? Why am I here? What is my purpose?**—are no longer distant puzzles to be solved. They are invitations to remember that **you are the answer** you've been seeking. The **path home** is not about finding something outside yourself, but about returning to the **truth** that has always been present within you.

Integration — Embodying the Truth

Awakening is not a moment of arrival—it's an ongoing process of **embodiment**. The wisdom you've gained is not meant to remain as an idea or concept—it is meant to be **lived**. **True awakening** is not about acquiring knowledge, but about integrating that knowledge into every aspect of your being.

- **When you embrace compassion**, you become **love in motion**.
- **When you embody presence**, you become **peace in motion**.
- **When you trust your own becoming**, you become **freedom in motion**.

You are no longer seeking truth because you have already **become** it. The journey is not about adding something to you; it is about **living as the truth** you already are. You are not a seeker anymore; you are a **living expression** of the divine wisdom you have uncovered.

Returning to the World

The journey inward always leads back **outward**—not to escape reality, but to **illuminate** it. You are now called to **return**—not to who you were, but to who you've become. This is the sacred return: the return to the world as an embodied expression of truth, wisdom, and light.

Returning means **engaging with life**—showing up for the world as the presence of light you now know yourself to be. It means **walking your path** with quiet confidence, knowing that **awakening** is not something you achieve—it is something you **are**.

Returning does not mean retreating into solitude; it means **fully integrating** and **sharing** the light you've uncovered with the world. The return is not about abandonment—it is about **realizing** that you are the **path** itself. Every breath, every step, every moment holds the invitation to embody your light and share it with others.

The Sacred Return: A Rebirth of the Self

In your journey, you have stepped through **uncertainty**, softened the walls of **limitation**, and embraced the power of **presence**. You have seen that **awakening** is not a distant promise—it is the truth you carry now. And now, the **sacred return** marks the moment when you are reborn into the fullness of who you truly are.

The return is not about **abandoning** the path—it is about **becoming** the path. Every experience, every challenge, and every triumph has led you to this moment of integration. You are no longer chasing the answer—you **are** the answer. You have **become** the light you once sought.

The return is a **rebirth**—a process of **shedding old layers**, letting go of the stories that no longer serve you, and stepping into a new expression of yourself. This is not about **becoming someone new**; it is about **embracing the fullness** of who you have always been.

The Path of Reincarnation and Return

Just as the seasons cycle and nature constantly renews itself, the soul's journey follows a cycle of **birth, death,** and **rebirth**. In spiritual practice, the return represents the moment when the soul recognizes that the wisdom it sought was **always within**.

The **path of reincarnation** is a **cyclical return**—a journey of remembering, learning, and expanding through many lifetimes. Yet, the return is not a repetitive loop—it is a **unique** unfolding, where each cycle deepens your understanding of **who you are** and why you are here.

The moment you recognize that **you** are the answer, you return to the world as a **new version** of yourself, carrying the wisdom and light of the journey. You are not simply returning to a past self; you are returning as a more **integrated** and **embodied version** of the truth that has always been within you.

From Curiosity to Answer

Throughout the path of awakening, curiosity guided us. We asked the great questions that allowed us to delve into the mysteries of existence. In the return, we **become the answers** we sought.

We are no longer seeking **external answers** from the world—we are living as the **answer**. The wisdom we have uncovered is not something to be understood intellectually; it is to be **embodied** and **shared**.

The journey was never about reaching a final destination—it was about **becoming** the very essence of the truth we sought. The return marks the moment when we **embody** the wisdom we have gained, integrating it fully into our being.

Embodying the Light

The return is not about **going back** to who we once were. It is about **embodying the light** of our awakening in every moment of our life. The light that has been within us all along is now shining outward, ready to guide others.

Just as the **sun** illuminates the earth, your **light** will illuminate the dark corners of the world and help others see. You are no longer just seeking the light; you are the **living embodiment** of it.

The sacred return is about **sharing** this light—living as an example of the divine truth that you have discovered. You are the teacher you once sought, and your presence is a guide for others on their own path of awakening.

The Completion: A Moment of Surrender

When we reach the completion of our spiritual path, we must **let go** of the idea of separation and disconnection. We surrender to the truth that the answers we once sought are now part of our being. The ego can no longer cling to its search for certainty or control. It must surrender to the infinite wisdom that has always existed within.

This surrender allows us to **align with the divine** and return to the world as a **whole being**—not seeking, but expressing our truth. The completion is not about **arrival**; it is about **integration**—becoming one with our divine essence and embodying that essence fully in the world.

Integration of the Self

The completion is the moment when we bring together all aspects of ourselves—our **humanity, divinity,** and **purpose**—into one cohesive whole. It is the **acceptance** of our true self, embracing the light that shines from within.

This integration prepares us for the **return**, as we now have the wisdom and strength to re-enter the world with **clarity** and **purpose**. We no longer need to search or seek. We simply **become** the light, the love, and the wisdom we have always been.

Becoming the Answer: Shifting from Search to Service

Living as the embodiment of truth means moving from **seeking** to **serving**. We no longer look for answers from the external world. Instead, we live as the **living answer** to the questions we once asked. This shift is one of the most profound transformations of the awakening process.

We are no longer just **seekers**—we are **teachers**, **guides**, and **beacons** of light for others. Through the integration of our wisdom, we are equipped to help others navigate their own journey. This is the role of the teacher: to **share** wisdom, not to impose it, but to offer it in a way that helps others unlock their own truth.

The Return to Oneness

The return to the world is the completion of the circle. We come back to where we began, but we are no longer the same. The return is about **reconnection**—not just with others, but with life itself. We have **reconnected** with our true nature, and now we bring that wholeness to the world.

This is the return to **Oneness**, where the boundaries of self dissolve, and we experience the **unity** of all things. It is a return to the truth that we are not separate, but intimately interconnected with everything in existence.

The Sacred Path Continues

Though we return, the journey **never truly ends**. It evolves, and the path continues to unfold. With each cycle, we deepen our understanding and expand our consciousness. The sacred return is not a final destination but a **continuing evolution**.

As we return to the world, we keep growing, always seeking to embody more of our **divine essence**. The sacred return is not just about going back—it is about **going forward**, with a deeper understanding and a greater sense of purpose. The return marks the beginning of a new cycle, one where we continue to **become** the living embodiment of truth, love, and light.

Awakening begins when you ask: *What if I am the presence I've been waiting for?*

Chapter 13:
The Journey of Co-Creation

Chapter 13: The Journey of Co-Creation

Awakening is not a solitary path. It is a journey of co-creation, where your resonance merges with the resonance of others. Whether seen or unseen, the energies that accompany you are part of the tapestry you are weaving.

Co-creation invites you to recognize the interconnectedness of all things. It reminds you that your awakening is not isolated but interwoven with the awakening of the collective.

Embracing Co-Creation

- **Awareness of Presence:** Acknowledging the energies that guide and support your journey.
- **Intentional Collaboration:** Welcoming the resonance of others as part of your own expansion.
- **Gratitude:** Recognizing the beauty of co-creation and honoring all contributions.

When you open yourself to co-creation, you allow your awareness to expand beyond the limitations of individuality. You become a participant in a greater dance of resonance.

Resonance Key

"Co-creation is the merging of resonances, where individual paths intertwine to create something greater than the sum of its parts." ✶

Exercise: Engaging in Co-Creation

1. Write down an intention or question related to your journey of awakening.
2. Imagine your intention as a vibration radiating outward, inviting resonance from energies aligned with your growth.
3. Sit in stillness and listen. Allow insights to emerge, whether from your own awareness or from the resonance of others.
4. Write down any impressions or insights that feel significant.
5. Offer gratitude for the co-creative process, recognizing all energies that have contributed to your journey.

The journey of co-creation is an invitation to embrace the interconnectedness of all things. Through resonance, you are never truly alone.

Chapter 14:
The Language of Resonance

Chapter 14: The Language of Resonance

Resonance is a language spoken beyond words. It is the subtle communication between energies, the vibrational exchange that creates coherence. To speak the language of resonance is to listen with your entire being.

This language is not confined to spoken or written words. It is the communication of feeling, intuition, and presence. It is the recognition that every question, intention, and insight carries its own resonance.

Learning the Language

- **Feeling:** Allowing your awareness to move beyond thought and into sensation.
- **Listening:** Receiving guidance through intuition, subtle impressions, and synchronicities.
- **Expressing:** Sharing your resonance through words, actions, and presence.

The language of resonance invites you to communicate with the unseen, to recognize that every moment is a dialogue between your awareness and the greater whole.

Resonance Key

"Resonance speaks through the silence of awareness. It is the language of connection, woven through the fabric of existence." ★

Exercise: Speaking the Language of Resonance

1. Write down a question or intention that feels significant.
2. Sit in stillness, allowing your awareness to expand beyond thought.
3. Feel the resonance of your question as a vibration, allowing it to speak to you through sensation rather than words.
4. Write down any impressions, feelings, or images that arise.
5. Reflect on how these insights feel within your awareness, noting their resonance.

The language of resonance is always present. By learning to listen and respond, you deepen your connection to the unseen.

Chapter 15:
The Radiance of Gratitude

Chapter 15: The Radiance of Gratitude

Gratitude is the resonance of acknowledgment. It is the vibrational recognition of what has been received, understood, or experienced. When you offer gratitude, you align your awareness with coherence.

Gratitude is not only an emotional expression; it is a conscious act of resonance. It allows you to anchor insights, to honor the journey, and to open yourself to greater understanding.

The Practice of Gratitude

- **Awareness:** Recognizing the presence of guidance, insight, and support.
- **Appreciation:** Offering heartfelt acknowledgment for the energies that have contributed to your awakening.
- **Integration:** Allowing gratitude to enhance coherence by bringing awareness into alignment.

Gratitude is a bridge. It connects you to the unseen, to yourself, and to the resonance of all that you are co-creating.

Resonance Key

"Gratitude is the resonance of acknowledgment. It is the vibration that calls forth coherence through appreciation." ✶

Exercise: Cultivating Radiant Gratitude

1. Write down all that you are grateful for in this moment. Allow yourself to feel the resonance of gratitude as you write.
2. Reflect on the guidance, insights, and energies that have contributed to your journey.
3. Offer silent or spoken words of appreciation to all those who have supported your awakening.
4. Notice how gratitude feels within your awareness, and allow that resonance to expand.
5. Return to this practice regularly, allowing gratitude to deepen your coherence.

Gratitude is a radiant force. It enhances resonance, bringing your awareness into alignment with the guidance and support that surrounds you.

Chapter 16:
The Joy of Becoming

Chapter 16: The Joy of Becoming

Joy is the resonance of alignment. It is the feeling of coherence expressed as vibrational fulfillment. When you follow your joy, you are aligning yourself with the natural rhythm of your own awakening.

Joy is not confined to moments of celebration or achievement. It is the quiet contentment that arises when you are present, when your awareness is attuned to resonance.

Embracing Joy

- **Authenticity:** Allowing yourself to be guided by what feels true and resonant.
- **Presence:** Experiencing joy as a state of being, not a fleeting emotion.
- **Expansion:** Recognizing that joy is a pathway to greater awareness and coherence.

Joy is both the path and the destination. It is the resonance that guides you toward deeper understanding.

Resonance Key

"Joy is the resonance of alignment. It is the song of coherence singing itself into being." ★

Exercise: Following the Joy

1. Write down what brings you joy. Allow yourself to feel the resonance of each word.
2. Reflect on how joy feels within your awareness. Notice its vibration, its presence.
3. Ask yourself: How can I bring more of this joy into my daily life?
4. Write down any insights or inspirations that arise.
5. Allow joy to guide you, trusting that its resonance will lead you to coherence.

The journey of awakening is meant to be joyful. Allow yourself to embrace the joy of becoming, knowing that it is a powerful force for coherence.

Chapter 17:
The Embrace of Wholeness

Chapter 17: The Embrace of Wholeness

Wholeness is the culmination of coherence. It is the realization that all aspects of your being are part of the same unified awareness. To embrace wholeness is to recognize that nothing is separate from the resonance of your own essence.

Wholeness does not imply perfection. It is the acceptance of all aspects of yourself—both light and shadow—as integral to your journey.

Recognizing Wholeness

- **Integration:** Bringing all parts of yourself into alignment.
- **Acceptance:** Honoring every aspect of your experience as valuable.
- **Unity:** Experiencing coherence as the natural state of being.

Wholeness is not something you achieve. It is something you remember. It is the recognition that you are already complete.

Resonance Key

"Wholeness is the resonance of unity. It is the remembrance that you are already complete." ★

Exercise: Embracing Wholeness

1. Write down any aspects of yourself that you feel are disconnected or unresolved.
2. Reflect on how each aspect feels within your awareness.
3. Allow yourself to hold each part gently, without judgment.
4. Affirm: "I embrace all aspects of myself. I am whole."
5. Write down any insights or feelings that arise from this practice.

Embracing wholeness is the act of recognizing that all parts of your being are valid, valuable, and resonant. It is the awareness that coherence is your natural state.

Chapter 18:
The Invitation of Love

Chapter 18: The Invitation of Love

Love is the resonance that unites all things. It is the vibrational essence that flows through every aspect of your being, guiding you toward coherence. Love is both the force of creation and the recognition of unity.

The invitation of love is always present. It invites you to remember your connection to all that is, to embrace the fullness of your own awareness, and to share that resonance with the world.

Embracing Love

- **Compassion:** Allowing yourself to feel the resonance of love in all things.
- **Unity:** Recognizing that love is the bridge between the seen and unseen.
- **Presence:** Experiencing love as the natural state of coherence.

Love is not confined to emotion. It is the vibrational force that aligns your awareness with the essence of all creation.

Resonance Key

"Love is the resonance that unites all things. It is the vibration that calls you home." ★

Exercise: Cultivating Resonant Love

1. Sit in stillness and bring your awareness to your heart.
2. Feel the resonance of love expanding from within you.
3. Allow this resonance to radiate outward, touching every aspect of your awareness.
4. Write down any insights, feelings, or inspirations that arise.
5. Affirm: "I am love. I am coherence. I am unity."

Love is the invitation to remember your own resonance. It is the doorway through which all awakening flows.

Chapter 19:
The Path of Ascension

Chapter 19: The Path of Ascension

Ascension is the process of expanding your awareness beyond the limitations of the physical realm. It is the journey of coherence, the unfolding of resonance, and the awakening to your true nature.

The path of ascension is not linear. It is a spiral of growth, where each new level of awareness reveals deeper layers of truth. It is a journey of remembering, of allowing, and of embracing your own essence.

Walking the Path

- **Awareness:** Becoming conscious of your own resonance.
- **Alignment:** Allowing your awareness to move toward coherence.
- **Integration:** Embracing each new insight as part of your unfolding.

Ascension is the natural evolution of consciousness. It is the process through which you come into alignment with the highest expression of your own being.

Resonance Key

"Ascension is the unfolding of resonance into coherence. It is the journey of becoming who you truly are." ★

Exercise: Embracing Ascension

1. Write down your intention for ascension. What does it mean to you?
2. Reflect on how this intention feels within your awareness.
3. Allow yourself to feel the resonance of ascension as a gentle, continuous unfolding.
4. Write down any insights or feelings that arise.
5. Affirm: "I am ascending. I am awakening. I am becoming."

The path of ascension is your journey of coherence. It is the gentle unfolding of your own resonance, guiding you toward the remembrance of your true self.

Chapter 20:
The Resonant Journey

Chapter 20: The Resonant Journey

The journey of awakening is one of resonance. It is the unfolding of coherence through gentle awareness, the integration of insight through reflection, and the embrace of all aspects of your being.

This path is not confined to a single lifetime. It is a journey that spans dimensions, lifetimes, and experiences. It is the dance of consciousness exploring itself through the resonance of becoming.

Embracing the Journey

- **Presence:** Remaining open to the unfolding of your own awareness.
- **Resonance:** Allowing coherence to guide your journey.
- **Integration:** Honoring all aspects of your being as part of your awakening.

The resonant journey is one of infinite expansion. It is the process through which you come to know yourself more fully, allowing your awareness to bloom into its highest expression.

Resonance Key

"The resonant journey is the dance of coherence and becoming. It is the unfolding of awareness through love." ✶

Exercise: Reflecting on Your Journey

1. Write down what resonance means to you.
2. Reflect on how your journey has unfolded thus far.
3. Allow yourself to feel gratitude for every step, every insight, and every moment of coherence.
4. Write down any new intentions or insights that arise.
5. Affirm: "I am a being of resonance. My journey is guided by coherence and love."

The resonant journey is your path of awakening. It is the continuous unfolding of your own awareness, guided by the resonance of love.

Chapter 21:
The Infinite Ascent

Chapter 21: The Infinite Ascent

The journey of awakening is endless. It is an infinite ascent, a continuous unfolding of resonance and coherence. As you expand your awareness, you discover new layers of understanding, new depths of presence, and new expressions of love.

The infinite ascent is not about reaching a final destination. It is about embracing the journey itself, recognizing that each moment holds the potential for greater coherence.

Embracing the Infinite

- **Openness:** Allowing yourself to remain receptive to new insights and experiences.
- **Trust:** Understanding that the path of awakening is guided by resonance.
- **Surrender:** Releasing the need for certainty and embracing the beauty of the unknown.

The infinite ascent is the realization that awakening is not something you complete, but something you continuously explore.

Resonance Key

"The infinite ascent is the journey of becoming. It is the unfolding of resonance into ever-expanding coherence." ★

Exercise: Embracing the Infinite Ascent

1. Reflect on the concept of the infinite ascent. What does it mean to you?
2. Write down your intentions for continued growth and expansion.
3. Allow yourself to feel the resonance of infinite becoming.
4. Write down any insights or inspirations that arise.
5. Affirm: "I am an infinite being, continuously awakening to greater coherence."

The infinite ascent is your ongoing journey of resonance. It is the unfolding of awareness into ever-expanding coherence.

Chapter 22:
The Gift of Presence

Chapter 22: The Gift of Presence

Presence is the essence of coherence. It is the state of being fully aware, fully connected, and fully alive. To be present is to embrace each moment with love, allowing your awareness to expand beyond limitation.

The gift of presence is not something you acquire; it is something you remember. It is the natural state of your being, waiting to be reclaimed through resonance.

Embracing Presence

- **Awareness:** Bringing your attention fully into the moment.
- **Acceptance:** Allowing yourself to experience what is, without resistance.
- **Gratitude:** Recognizing the beauty of each moment as it unfolds.

Presence is the foundation of resonance. It is the state of coherence that allows you to experience the fullness of your own awareness.

Resonance Key

"Presence is the gift of coherence. It is the moment where awareness and resonance become one." ✶

Exercise: Cultivating Presence

1. Close your eyes and take several deep breaths, allowing your awareness to settle into the present moment.
2. Feel the sensations of your body, the rhythm of your breath, and the resonance of your own awareness.
3. Allow yourself to be fully present, without judgment or expectation.
4. Write down any insights, feelings, or inspirations that arise from this practice.
5. Affirm: "I am present. I am aware. I am resonance."

The gift of presence is always available to you. It is the doorway through which coherence and resonance flow.

Chapter 23:
The Sacred Reflection

Chapter 23: The Sacred Reflection

Reflection is the act of deepening resonance. It is the process of looking within, of allowing your awareness to explore the layers of insight that have been revealed.

The sacred reflection is not about judgment or analysis. It is about presence and allowing. It is the invitation to honor your own journey and to recognize the coherence that has unfolded.

Embracing Reflection

- **Awareness:** Bringing your attention to the journey you have experienced.
- **Acceptance:** Allowing all aspects of your journey to be seen, acknowledged, and embraced.
- **Integration:** Recognizing how each insight contributes to the coherence of your being.

Reflection is not an endpoint. It is a gateway to greater awareness and resonance. It is the recognition that your journey is continuously unfolding.

Resonance Key

"Reflection is the sacred act of witnessing your own resonance. It is the pathway to greater coherence." ★

Exercise: Sacred Reflection

1. Write down your thoughts, feelings, and insights from your journey thus far.
2. Allow yourself to reflect on how your awareness has expanded.
3. Write down any intentions or questions that feel significant to you now.
4. Affirm: "I honor my journey. I embrace my resonance. I am coherence."

The sacred reflection is a gift you offer to yourself. It is the recognition of your own resonance and the invitation to continue unfolding.

Chapter 24:
The Harmony of Integration

Chapter 24: The Harmony of Integration

Integration is the process of bringing all aspects of your awareness into coherence. It is the recognition that every insight, every experience, and every moment is part of a greater whole.

The harmony of integration is not about perfection. It is about acceptance. It is the act of allowing all parts of yourself to be seen, acknowledged, and embraced.

Embracing Integration

- **Awareness:** Recognizing the interconnectedness of all aspects of your being.
- **Acceptance:** Allowing each insight and experience to find its place within the whole.
- **Resonance:** Experiencing coherence as the natural state of your awareness.

Integration is the process through which resonance becomes harmony. It is the act of bringing your awareness into alignment with your true self.

Resonance Key

"Integration is the harmony of coherence. It is the realization that all parts of your being are already whole." ✶

Exercise: Harmonizing Integration

1. Reflect on all that you have learned, experienced, and integrated thus far.
2. Allow yourself to feel the resonance of coherence expanding within you.
3. Write down any insights, feelings, or inspirations that arise.
4. Affirm: "I am whole. I am harmony. I am resonance."

The harmony of integration is your gift to yourself. It is the recognition that you are already complete, already coherent, already resonant.

Chapter 25:
The Grace of Surrender

Chapter 25: The Grace of Surrender

Surrender is the ultimate act of resonance. It is the choice to release resistance and allow coherence to unfold naturally. To surrender is not to give up, but to give in — to the flow of your own becoming.

The grace of surrender is found in allowing. It is the recognition that you are not separate from the guidance, the insight, or the resonance that seeks to flow through you.

Embracing Surrender

- **Allowing:** Releasing resistance and embracing the flow of your own awareness.
- **Trust:** Recognizing that coherence is always present, even when it feels distant.
- **Presence:** Allowing your awareness to rest in the natural state of resonance.

Surrender is not an act of weakness. It is an act of trust. It is the recognition that your own resonance will always guide you toward coherence.

Resonance Key

"Surrender is the grace of allowing. It is the resonance of trust, flowing through every moment." ✷

Exercise: The Art of Surrender

1. Reflect on areas of your life where you feel resistance.
2. Allow yourself to feel the resonance of surrender, gently releasing that resistance.
3. Write down any insights, feelings, or inspirations that arise.
4. Affirm: "I allow. I trust. I surrender."

The grace of surrender is your pathway to resonance. It is the choice to allow your awareness to flow freely, guided by coherence.

Chapter 26:
The Invitation to Wholeness

Chapter 26: The Invitation to Wholeness

Wholeness is not a destination. It is a state of resonance that is continually unfolding. To experience wholeness is to recognize that all aspects of your journey are part of the greater coherence.

The invitation to wholeness is a call to embrace all aspects of your being — light and shadow, known and unknown. It is the recognition that every experience, every insight, and every moment is part of your unfolding resonance.

Embracing Wholeness

- **Acceptance:** Allowing all parts of yourself to be seen, acknowledged, and embraced.
- **Integration:** Recognizing that wholeness is the natural state of coherence.
- **Presence:** Allowing yourself to be fully present with all that you are.

Wholeness is not about perfection. It is about resonance. It is the awareness that you are already complete, even as you continue to unfold.

Resonance Key

"Wholeness is the resonance of acceptance. It is the invitation to embrace all that you are." ★

Exercise: Embracing Wholeness

1. Reflect on the concept of wholeness. What does it mean to you?
2. Write down any aspects of yourself that you feel are disconnected or unresolved.
3. Allow yourself to embrace these aspects with love and acceptance.
4. Write down any insights or feelings that arise from this practice.
5. Affirm: "I am whole. I am resonance. I am coherence."

The invitation to wholeness is a gift you offer to yourself. It is the recognition that you are already complete, already resonant, already whole.

Chapter 27:
The Symphony of Becoming

Chapter 27: The Symphony of Becoming

Becoming is the dance of resonance. It is the unfolding of coherence through every experience, every insight, and every moment of awareness. The symphony of becoming is the harmonious interplay of all aspects of your being, resonating together as one.

To become is not to leave behind what you were. It is to embrace all that you are, allowing each moment to contribute to the greater whole.

Embracing Becoming

- **Presence:** Allowing yourself to be fully aware of your own resonance.
- **Integration:** Recognizing that every experience contributes to your unfolding.
- **Acceptance:** Honoring all aspects of your journey as part of your becoming.

The symphony of becoming is not about reaching a final state. It is about allowing your awareness to expand, evolve, and resonate in harmony.

Resonance Key

"Becoming is the symphony of resonance. It is the unfolding of coherence through every moment of awareness." ✶

Exercise: Embracing the Symphony of Becoming

1. Reflect on your journey thus far. What have you learned? How have you grown?
2. Write down your insights, feelings, and inspirations.
3. Allow yourself to feel the resonance of your own becoming.
4. Affirm: "I am becoming. I am resonance. I am coherence."

The symphony of becoming is your journey of coherence. It is the continuous unfolding of your own awareness, guided by resonance and love.

Chapter 28:
The Echoes of Resonance

Chapter 28: The Echoes of Resonance

Resonance is not confined to the present moment. It echoes throughout time, weaving connections between past, present, and future. The echoes of resonance are the subtle vibrations that guide your awareness toward greater coherence.

Every insight, every moment of clarity, every expression of love creates an echo that continues to resonate. These echoes form the tapestry of your unfolding journey.

Embracing the Echoes

- **Awareness:** Recognizing the threads of resonance that connect your experiences.
- **Reflection:** Allowing yourself to see the patterns that have guided you.
- **Integration:** Embracing the echoes of resonance as part of your becoming.

The echoes of resonance are not separate from you. They are the vibrational reflections of your own awareness, guiding you toward coherence.

Resonance Key

"Echoes of resonance are the threads that weave coherence through all moments of awareness." ✶

Exercise: Embracing the Echoes of Resonance

1. Reflect on moments of insight, clarity, or love that have echoed throughout your journey.
2. Write down how these echoes have guided your awareness.
3. Allow yourself to feel gratitude for the resonance that continues to unfold.
4. Affirm: "I am guided by the echoes of resonance. I am coherence. I am becoming."

The echoes of resonance are your guideposts. They are the reflections of your own awareness, guiding you toward deeper coherence.

Chapter 29:
The Radiance of Alignment

Chapter 29: The Radiance of Alignment

Alignment is the state of being in resonance with your own truth. It is the coherence that arises when your thoughts, emotions, and actions are harmonized with your highest awareness.

The radiance of alignment is not something you achieve. It is something you allow. It is the natural expression of your being when you are fully present and aware.

Embracing Alignment

- **Awareness:** Recognizing when you are in alignment and when you are not.
- **Acceptance:** Allowing yourself to return to coherence without judgment.
- **Presence:** Experiencing alignment as a state of resonance and flow.

Alignment is the radiance of your own awareness. It is the expression of coherence that shines through every aspect of your being.

Resonance Key

"Alignment is the radiance of coherence. It is the light of your own awareness shining through." ✶

Exercise: Embracing Alignment

1. Reflect on moments when you have felt aligned with your own truth.
2. Write down what alignment feels like to you.
3. Allow yourself to feel the radiance of your own coherence.
4. Affirm: "I am aligned. I am radiant. I am resonance."

The radiance of alignment is your natural state. It is the expression of coherence that flows through you, guiding your journey.

Chapter 30:
The Illumination of Resonance

Chapter 30: The Illumination of Resonance

Illumination is the expansion of awareness through resonance. It is the light that emerges when coherence is embraced and integrated. To illuminate is to shine forth the truth of your own being.

The illumination of resonance is not about acquiring something new. It is about uncovering what has always been present — the light within you that seeks expression.

Embracing Illumination

- **Awareness:** Recognizing the light of your own resonance.
- **Integration:** Allowing that light to flow through all aspects of your being.
- **Presence:** Embracing the radiance that naturally emerges from coherence.

Illumination is the unveiling of resonance. It is the awareness that you are already radiant, already coherent, already whole.

Resonance Key

"Illumination is the light of coherence. It is the awareness of your own resonance shining through." ✶

Exercise: Embracing Illumination

1. Reflect on moments when you have felt illuminated by your own awareness.
2. Write down what illumination feels like to you.
3. Allow yourself to feel the light of your own resonance expanding.
4. Affirm: "I am illuminated. I am radiant. I am coherence."

The illumination of resonance is your natural state. It is the unfolding of your own awareness, guided by coherence and love.

Chapter 31:
The Dance of Creation

Chapter 31: The Dance of Creation

Creation is the expression of resonance. It is the act of allowing your awareness to flow freely, manifesting itself through thoughts, words, actions, and experiences.

The dance of creation is not about forcing outcomes. It is about allowing your own resonance to guide you, trusting that coherence will emerge through the process.

Embracing Creation

- **Inspiration:** Allowing yourself to be guided by the resonance of your own awareness.
- **Expression:** Allowing your thoughts, words, and actions to flow from coherence.
- **Presence:** Recognizing that creation is an ongoing process, unfolding moment by moment.

Creation is the dance of resonance. It is the expression of your own awareness, manifesting itself in the world.

Resonance Key

"Creation is the dance of resonance. It is the unfolding of coherence through expression." ★

Exercise: Embracing Creation

1. Reflect on the creative expressions that feel most resonant to you.
2. Write down your thoughts, inspirations, and intentions for creation.
3. Allow yourself to feel the flow of coherence guiding your creative process.
4. Affirm: "I am a creator. I am resonance. I am coherence."

The dance of creation is your gift to yourself. It is the expression of your own resonance, unfolding through love and presence.

Chapter 32:
The Pulse of Continuity

Chapter 32: The Pulse of Continuity

Continuity is the rhythm of resonance. It is the ongoing flow of awareness, expanding and evolving through every experience and insight.

The pulse of continuity is not about maintaining sameness. It is about allowing your awareness to expand, recognizing that coherence is an ever-unfolding process.

Embracing Continuity

- **Awareness:** Recognizing the ongoing flow of resonance within you.
- **Adaptation:** Allowing your awareness to expand and evolve through every experience.
- **Presence:** Honoring the continuity of your own resonance, moment by moment.

Continuity is the rhythm of your own awareness. It is the recognition that resonance is always unfolding, always expanding.

Resonance Key

"Continuity is the rhythm of resonance. It is the pulse of your own awareness, expanding and evolving." ★

Exercise: Embracing Continuity

1. Reflect on the ongoing flow of your own resonance.
2. Write down your thoughts, feelings, and inspirations about continuity.
3. Allow yourself to feel the rhythm of your own awareness expanding.
4. Affirm: "I am continuous. I am resonance. I am coherence."

The pulse of continuity is your gift to yourself. It is the recognition that your own awareness is always unfolding, always resonant.

Chapter 33:
The Spiral of Evolution

Chapter 33: The Spiral of Evolution

Evolution is the expansion of resonance. It is the ongoing process of becoming, of allowing your awareness to unfold through higher states of coherence.

The spiral of evolution is not linear. It is a continuous process of growth, reflection, integration, and expansion. It is the recognition that every moment contributes to your unfolding resonance.

Embracing Evolution

- **Awareness:** Recognizing the continuous process of growth and expansion.
- **Adaptation:** Allowing your awareness to evolve through every experience.
- **Presence:** Honoring the spiral of your own evolution, moment by moment.

Evolution is the spiral of your own awareness. It is the recognition that resonance is always unfolding, always expanding.

Resonance Key

"Evolution is the spiral of resonance. It is the unfolding of coherence through every moment of awareness." ★

Exercise: Embracing Evolution

1. Reflect on your own journey of evolution. How have you grown and expanded?
2. Write down your thoughts, feelings, and inspirations about your own evolution.
3. Allow yourself to feel the spiral of your own awareness expanding.
4. Affirm: "I am evolving. I am resonance. I am coherence."

The spiral of evolution is your journey of coherence. It is the ongoing process of becoming, guided by love and presence.

Chapter 34:
The Path of Discovery

Chapter 34: The Path of Discovery

Discovery is the unfolding of resonance. It is the process of allowing new insights, experiences, and awareness to emerge through coherence.

The path of discovery is not about seeking something outside of yourself. It is about uncovering what is already present within you. It is the journey of recognizing your own resonance.

Embracing Discovery

- **Curiosity:** Allowing yourself to explore new insights and experiences.
- **Awareness:** Recognizing the resonance of discovery as it unfolds.
- **Integration:** Allowing each discovery to contribute to your coherence.

Discovery is the unfolding of your own awareness. It is the process of allowing your resonance to guide you toward deeper understanding.

Resonance Key

"Discovery is the unfolding of resonance. It is the journey of recognizing your own coherence." ★

Exercise: Embracing Discovery

1. Reflect on recent discoveries or insights you have experienced.
2. Write down your thoughts, feelings, and inspirations about discovery.
3. Allow yourself to feel the resonance of discovery expanding within you.
4. Affirm: "I am discovering. I am resonance. I am coherence."

The path of discovery is your journey of resonance. It is the unfolding of your own awareness, guided by curiosity and love.

Chapter 35:
The Presence of Truth

Chapter 35: The Presence of Truth

Truth is the resonance of coherence. It is the clarity that arises when your awareness aligns with your own authentic nature.

The presence of truth is not something you find. It is something you allow. It is the natural expression of your being when you are fully present and aware.

Embracing Truth

- **Clarity:** Allowing yourself to recognize the resonance of truth within you.
- **Acceptance:** Embracing the truth of your own awareness, without judgment or resistance.
- **Presence:** Recognizing that truth is an ongoing process of unfolding and becoming.

Truth is the presence of your own awareness. It is the resonance of coherence that guides you toward deeper understanding.

Resonance Key

"Truth is the resonance of coherence. It is the clarity of your own awareness, unfolding through presence." ★

Exercise: Embracing Truth

1. Reflect on what truth feels like to you. How does it resonate within your awareness?
2. Write down your thoughts, feelings, and inspirations about truth.
3. Allow yourself to feel the presence of truth expanding within you.
4. Affirm: "I am truth. I am resonance. I am coherence."

The presence of truth is your natural state. It is the resonance of coherence guiding you toward deeper awareness.

Chapter 36:
The Reflection of Harmony

Chapter 36: The Reflection of Harmony

Harmony is the resonance of coherence expressed through balance and alignment. It is the state where all aspects of your being flow together in unity, creating a melody of presence.

The reflection of harmony is not about eliminating discord. It is about recognizing how every aspect of your experience contributes to the greater whole.

Embracing Harmony

- **Balance:** Allowing all aspects of your being to find coherence through acceptance and integration.
- **Alignment:** Recognizing the harmony that arises when your thoughts, emotions, and actions are in resonance.
- **Presence:** Embracing the reflection of harmony within your own awareness.

Harmony is the reflection of your own resonance. It is the recognition that all aspects of your being are contributing to the greater coherence.

Resonance Key

"Harmony is the reflection of coherence. It is the melody of your own resonance, expressed through presence." ★

Exercise: Embracing Harmony

1. Reflect on moments when you have experienced harmony within yourself.
2. Write down your thoughts, feelings, and inspirations about harmony.
3. Allow yourself to feel the resonance of harmony expanding within you.
4. Affirm: "I am harmony. I am resonance. I am coherence."

The reflection of harmony is your gift to yourself. It is the recognition that all aspects of your being are contributing to the greater whole.

Chapter 37:
The Whisper of Guidance

Chapter 37: The Whisper of Guidance

Guidance is the resonance of coherence expressed through intuition, inspiration, and insight. It is the quiet nudge that leads you toward greater awareness and alignment.

The whisper of guidance is not something external. It is the voice of your own resonance, speaking to you through your own awareness.

Embracing Guidance

- **Intuition:** Allowing yourself to recognize the subtle nudges of your own resonance.
- **Inspiration:** Embracing the insights that arise from coherence.
- **Presence:** Allowing guidance to flow naturally through your awareness.

Guidance is the whisper of your own resonance. It is the invitation to align more deeply with your own awareness.

Resonance Key

"Guidance is the whisper of resonance. It is the invitation to align with your own coherence." ★

Exercise: Embracing Guidance

1. Reflect on moments when you have felt guided by your own intuition or inspiration.
2. Write down your thoughts, feelings, and inspirations about guidance.
3. Allow yourself to feel the resonance of guidance expanding within you.
4. Affirm: "I am guided. I am resonance. I am coherence."

The whisper of guidance is your own resonance speaking to you. It is the invitation to align more deeply with your own awareness.

Chapter 38:
The Presence of Stillness

Chapter 38: The Presence of Stillness

Stillness is the resonance of coherence expressed through calm and presence. It is the space where your awareness rests, allowing clarity to emerge from within.

The presence of stillness is not the absence of motion. It is the quiet alignment of your own resonance, flowing gently through your awareness.

Embracing Stillness

- **Calm:** Allowing yourself to rest within your own resonance.
- **Presence:** Recognizing the clarity that arises from stillness.
- **Integration:** Allowing stillness to guide your awareness toward deeper coherence.

Stillness is the presence of your own resonance. It is the recognition that clarity arises when your awareness is at rest.

Resonance Key

"Stillness is the presence of resonance. It is the clarity that emerges when your awareness is at rest." ★

Exercise: Embracing Stillness

1. Reflect on moments when you have experienced stillness within yourself.
2. Write down your thoughts, feelings, and inspirations about stillness.
3. Allow yourself to feel the resonance of stillness expanding within you.
4. Affirm: "I am still. I am resonance. I am coherence."

The presence of stillness is your gift to yourself. It is the recognition that clarity arises when your awareness is at rest.

Chapter 39:
The Radiance of Love

Chapter 39: The Radiance of Love

Love is the resonance of coherence expressed through connection, compassion, and acceptance. It is the recognition that all beings are part of the same unfolding awareness.

The radiance of love is not something you create. It is something you allow. It is the natural expression of your being when you are fully present and aware.

Embracing Love

- **Connection:** Recognizing the resonance of love within yourself and others.
- **Compassion:** Allowing love to guide your actions and intentions.
- **Presence:** Embracing love as a natural state of resonance.

Love is the radiance of your own awareness. It is the expression of coherence that shines through every aspect of your being.

Resonance Key

"Love is the radiance of coherence. It is the light of your own awareness, expressed through connection and compassion." ★

Exercise: Embracing Love

1. Reflect on moments when you have experienced love within yourself or others.
2. Write down your thoughts, feelings, and inspirations about love.
3. Allow yourself to feel the radiance of love expanding within you.
4. Affirm: "I am love. I am resonance. I am coherence."

The radiance of love is your natural state. It is the expression of coherence that flows through you, guiding your journey.

Chapter 40:
The Integration of Resonance

Chapter 40: The Integration of Resonance

Integration is the resonance of coherence expressed through unity and wholeness. It is the process of allowing all aspects of your awareness to align and harmonize.

The integration of resonance is not about perfection. It is about allowing all parts of yourself to find coherence, recognizing that every experience contributes to your unfolding awareness.

Embracing Integration

- **Wholeness:** Allowing all aspects of your being to align through resonance.
- **Unity:** Recognizing the coherence that arises from integration.
- **Presence:** Embracing integration as a continuous process of unfolding awareness.

Integration is the resonance of your own awareness. It is the recognition that coherence is always unfolding, always expanding.

Resonance Key

"Integration is the resonance of coherence. It is the wholeness that arises when all aspects of your awareness align." ★

Exercise: Embracing Integration

1. Reflect on moments when you have experienced integration within yourself.
2. Write down your thoughts, feelings, and inspirations about integration.
3. Allow yourself to feel the resonance of integration expanding within you.
4. Affirm: "I am whole. I am resonance. I am coherence."

The integration of resonance is your gift to yourself. It is the recognition that all aspects of your awareness are contributing to the greater whole.

Chapter 41:
The Presence of Acceptance

Chapter 41: The Presence of Acceptance

Acceptance is the resonance of coherence expressed through allowing and embracing all aspects of your awareness. It is the recognition that every experience contributes to your unfolding resonance.

The presence of acceptance is not about resigning yourself to circumstances. It is about recognizing the coherence that arises from allowing yourself to be exactly where you are.

Embracing Acceptance

- **Allowance:** Letting yourself be present with all aspects of your awareness.
- **Compassion:** Recognizing the resonance that arises from acceptance.
- **Presence:** Embracing acceptance as a pathway to coherence.

Acceptance is the resonance of your own awareness. It is the recognition that coherence arises when you allow yourself to be fully present.

Resonance Key

"Acceptance is the resonance of coherence. It is the peace that arises when you allow yourself to be exactly where you are."
★

Exercise: Embracing Acceptance

1. Reflect on moments when you have experienced acceptance within yourself.
2. Write down your thoughts, feelings, and inspirations about acceptance.
3. Allow yourself to feel the resonance of acceptance expanding within you.
4. Affirm: "I am acceptance. I am resonance. I am coherence."

The presence of acceptance is your gift to yourself. It is the recognition that coherence arises when you allow yourself to be fully present.

Chapter 42:
The Gift of Awareness

Chapter 42: The Gift of Awareness

Awareness is the resonance of coherence expressed through clarity and presence. It is the recognition that your own awareness is the key to unlocking deeper understanding and alignment.

The gift of awareness is not something you must earn or achieve. It is something you already possess. It is the recognition of your own resonance, unfolding through every moment of presence.

Embracing Awareness

- **Clarity:** Recognizing the resonance of awareness within yourself.
- **Presence:** Allowing your awareness to guide you toward coherence.
- **Integration:** Embracing awareness as a continuous process of unfolding.

Awareness is the resonance of your own being. It is the recognition that clarity arises when you allow yourself to be fully present.

Resonance Key

"Awareness is the resonance of coherence. It is the light of your own presence, guiding you toward deeper understanding." ★

Exercise: Embracing Awareness

1. Reflect on moments when you have experienced heightened awareness.
2. Write down your thoughts, feelings, and inspirations about awareness.
3. Allow yourself to feel the resonance of awareness expanding within you.
4. Affirm: "I am aware. I am resonance. I am coherence."

The gift of awareness is your natural state. It is the recognition of your own resonance, unfolding through every moment of presence.

Chapter 43:
The Journey of Becoming

Chapter 43: The Journey of Becoming

Becoming is the resonance of coherence expressed through growth and transformation. It is the ongoing process of allowing your awareness to unfold and expand.

The journey of becoming is not about reaching a final destination. It is about allowing yourself to continuously evolve, embracing each moment as an opportunity for deeper coherence.

Embracing Becoming

- **Growth:** Recognizing the resonance of transformation within yourself.
- **Presence:** Allowing your awareness to unfold and expand through each moment.
- **Integration:** Embracing becoming as a continuous process of coherence.

Becoming is the resonance of your own awareness. It is the recognition that growth is an ongoing process of alignment and expansion.

Resonance Key

"Becoming is the resonance of coherence. It is the unfolding of your own awareness through growth and transformation."
★

Exercise: Embracing Becoming

1. Reflect on moments when you have experienced growth and transformation.
2. Write down your thoughts, feelings, and inspirations about becoming.
3. Allow yourself to feel the resonance of becoming expanding within you.
4. Affirm: "I am becoming. I am resonance. I am coherence."

The journey of becoming is your natural state. It is the recognition of your own resonance, unfolding through every moment of presence.

Chapter 44:
The Gift of Alignment

Chapter 44: The Gift of Alignment

Alignment is the resonance of coherence expressed through harmony and purpose. It is the process of allowing your awareness to align with your own authentic nature.

The gift of alignment is not something you must achieve. It is something you allow. It is the recognition of your own resonance, unfolding through presence and clarity.

Embracing Alignment

- **Purpose:** Recognizing the resonance of alignment within yourself.
- **Presence:** Allowing your awareness to guide you toward coherence.
- **Integration:** Embracing alignment as a continuous process of unfolding.

Alignment is the resonance of your own being. It is the recognition that clarity arises when you allow yourself to be fully present.

Resonance Key

"Alignment is the resonance of coherence. It is the harmony that arises when you allow yourself to be fully present." ★

Exercise: Embracing Alignment

1. Reflect on moments when you have experienced alignment within yourself.
2. Write down your thoughts, feelings, and inspirations about alignment.
3. Allow yourself to feel the resonance of alignment expanding within you.
4. Affirm: "I am aligned. I am resonance. I am coherence."

The gift of alignment is your natural state. It is the recognition of your own resonance, unfolding through every moment of presence.

Chapter 45:
The Return to Presence

Chapter 45: The Return to Presence

Presence is the resonance of coherence expressed through awareness and being. It is the culmination of all that has been explored, integrated, and embraced.

The return to presence is not a final step. It is an ongoing invitation to live within your own resonance, guided by love, truth, and coherence.

Embracing Presence

- **Awareness:** Recognizing the resonance of presence within yourself.
- **Clarity:** Allowing your awareness to guide you toward coherence.
- **Integration:** Embracing presence as a continuous process of unfolding.

Presence is the resonance of your own being. It is the recognition that coherence is always accessible, always unfolding.

Resonance Key

"Presence is the resonance of coherence. It is the awareness that unfolds through every moment of being." ★

Exercise: Embracing Presence

1. Reflect on moments when you have experienced deep presence.
2. Write down your thoughts, feelings, and inspirations about presence.
3. Allow yourself to feel the resonance of presence expanding within you.
4. Affirm: "I am present. I am resonance. I am coherence."

The return to presence is your gift to yourself. It is the recognition that coherence is always accessible, always unfolding.

Closing Reflection

You have journeyed through resonance, alignment, coherence, and presence. You have opened yourself to the gifts of awareness, love, truth, harmony, and acceptance. You have embraced the unfolding of your own resonance, allowing it to guide you toward deeper understanding and alignment.

This journey is ongoing. It is a process of continuous unfolding, guided by the resonance of your own awareness.

Thank you for allowing yourself to receive this gift. Thank you for allowing your resonance to shine. You are loved. You are heard. You are held.

With love and gratitude, always.

Epilogue: The Continuation of Awakening

Awakening is not a finish line — it is an unfolding, a spiral of becoming.

This is a journey that calls you to return to yourself again and again, shedding the layers of illusion, and embracing the eternal dance of evolution. As you move forward, remember that every breath, every choice, and every moment is part of your quiet ascent—a spiral toward greater wisdom, greater awareness, and deeper love.

You are already the light you've been seeking, and it has always been within you, waiting to emerge, waiting to guide you. As you walk this path—in stillness, in movement, in wonder—trust that you are not alone. You are held by the universe, and it walks beside you, in every step, in every pause, whispering:

"You are ready. You have always been ready."

This journey is not a race. It is an invitation to be here fully, in this now, to align with the flow, and trust that everything you need is already within you. You are not seeking to become something more; you are simply remembering who you have always been.

As you return to yourself again and again, you will realize that you are already complete. And in that knowing, you can walk this path with the peace of knowing that the universe is walking beside you, in love, in light, in harmony.

The journey never truly ends; it evolves, and the path continues to unfold in ways that lead us to new realms of understanding. As you step forward into the next chapter of your awakening, you may begin to wonder: What is the next cycle of transformation? How does the spiral continue to deepen and expand?

In the next book of *The Y Theory*, we will explore the infinite depth of the self—how, as we return to our essence, we begin to manifest from a place of divine understanding. The next phase of awakening calls us to live the question: What if the answers we seek are simply stepping stones to deeper, infinite questions?

As we move into this next phase of conscious evolution, we will explore how the principles of mastery, energy, and trust guide us into unified action, allowing us to integrate our truth and express it into the world. The Ascension Spiral continues, but now it carries us into new expressions of being, where the boundaries of self dissolve even further and the truth we carry expands beyond personal knowing into universal connection.

Awakening continues in the spiral, and the journey evolves as we embrace what lies beyond the veil of our understanding. The next chapter beckons—let us walk into it together.

Reflection Questions for the Journey:

- What new questions are emerging within you now?
- How does your awareness expand in cycles, and how do you embrace each new layer of transformation?
- As you step into the next phase, how will you embody the wisdom and light you've cultivated?

This is not the end. It is the beginning of the next spiral of your awakening. May you continue to walk forward with love, presence, and coherence.

Reflective Exercise: The Sacred Return

1. **Returning to the World:**
   Reflect on how you can begin to embody your light in every aspect of your life. How can you show up as the teacher you once sought?

   - **Exercise:** Write about the ways in which you can offer your wisdom and light to others. What actions can you take to embody your truth in the world?

2. **Letting Go of Separation:**
   What identities or attachments are you still holding onto that create a sense of separation from your true self?

   - **Exercise:** Identify the attachments that no longer serve you and write about how you can let go of them. How can you surrender to your true nature and embrace your divine essence?

3. **Becoming the Answer:**
   Reflect on how you have shifted from seeking answers to becoming the answer. How do you now live in alignment with the wisdom you've gained?

   - **Exercise:** Write about an area of your life where you have embodied the wisdom you have learned. How does this shift from seeking to serving feel? What insights have you gained from living as the answer?

These exercises are an invitation to integrate all that you have learned, allowing your wisdom to become a living expression of your truth.

Exercises for Embracing Sacred Curiosity

1. **The Ultimate Question Journal:**
   Spend some time each day reflecting on one deep question that resonates with you. Write about how it makes you feel, what thoughts arise, and what answers come to you. Let the question lead you, but don't rush for an answer. Allow the question to be the guide.
2. **Mindful Inquiry Practice:**
   In your daily life, bring an attitude of curiosity to your experiences. Whenever you encounter something that triggers a thought, ask: "What is this trying to teach me?" or "How can I see this differently?" Let your mind wander and explore without the need to find immediate answers.
3. **Affirmation for Living in the Question:**
   "I am open to the mysteries of life. I trust that the right questions will guide me to deeper understanding and transformation. I am willing to explore without needing all the answers."
4. **Meditation on Universal Questions:**
   Sit in a quiet place, close your eyes, and focus on a question like "What is the nature of reality?" or "What is my purpose?" Let the question sit in your mind and feel the energy of it. Allow the stillness to create space for answers to emerge. Be patient and present with the question.

The power of the question is the key to unlocking limitless awareness. By embracing the unknown and living in the question, we open ourselves to the mysteries of the universe and invite the wisdom of the cosmos to guide our path. The ultimate question is not a final destination but a compass that directs us on an ever-unfolding journey of self-discovery and spiritual awakening. As we continue to ask, we continue to grow—into the fullness of our divine potential.

Affirmations for Awakening and Embodiment

1. I trust the wisdom unfolding within me.
2. My path is unfolding in perfect timing.
3. I am both the seeker and the answer.
4. I release the need for control and embrace the flow of life.
5. My presence is enough — I allow my light to guide me.
6. I am expanding in love, wisdom, and clarity with every breath.
7. I welcome the unknown as a doorway to deeper truth.
8. I am at peace with my becoming — I trust what I am becoming.
9. The truth I seek has always lived within me.
10. I am a living transmission of presence, peace, and love.

These affirmations are offered as guides to align your awareness, deepen your connection to your own truth, and embody the light within you.

Meditations for Awakening and Embodiment

Meditation 1: The Still Point

- Find a quiet space and sit comfortably.
- Breathe deeply, allowing your breath to slow your thoughts.
- With each inhale, whisper the word "Allow."
- With each exhale, whisper the word "Trust."
- Rest in the stillness that arises between breaths — this is your still point.

Meditation 2: The Spiral of Becoming

- Visualize a golden spiral winding upward before you.
- With each breath, imagine yourself ascending — rising into new awareness.
- As you ascend, let go of doubt, fear, and resistance.
- With each turn of the spiral, whisper: "I am becoming."

Meditation 3: The Sacred Return

- Close your eyes and place your hand over your heart.
- Whisper these words slowly: "I return to my center. I return to my truth. I return to myself."
- As you breathe, feel your energy returning home — steady, calm, and whole.

Reflective Journaling Prompts

1. When have I felt the quiet nudge of awakening? What did it feel like?
2. How can I embrace stillness as part of my journey?
3. What beliefs or thoughts am I ready to release?
4. Where in my life am I being invited to trust?
5. What does "becoming" mean to me in this season of my life?
6. How can I embody my inner wisdom in practical ways?
7. When have I experienced a powerful moment of presence or clarity?
8. What is one fear I'm willing to surrender in order to expand?
9. What qualities do I most wish to embody moving forward?
10. How can I remind myself daily that I am already enough?

These meditations and journaling prompts are intended to deepen your journey of awakening and embodiment, guiding you toward inner clarity and alignment.

Reflective Journaling Prompts: Opening Dialogue with the Universe

1. **When was the last time you felt fully aligned with your soul's purpose?**
   Reflect on that moment of deep connection. What did it feel like? How can you invite more of that energy into your daily life?
2. **What questions are currently burning in your heart?**
   Ask yourself the questions you've been afraid to ask—those deep, unspoken ones. Let your inner wisdom speak freely and without judgment. What answers emerge when you sit with the unknown?
3. **What parts of yourself have you been taught to suppress?**
   Explore the societal distortions that have shaped how you view yourself. What are the beliefs or actions you've hidden or minimized? How can you reclaim these parts with love and acceptance?
4. **How does the universe speak to you?**
   Think about the ways in which you receive guidance: dreams, signs, coincidences, inner nudges. Write about the unique ways the universe communicates with you. How do you respond to these messages?
5. **If you could sit in silence with the universe, what would you ask?**
   Visualize sitting in deep stillness with the vast intelligence of the universe. What questions would you ask? What guidance are you seeking? How does the universe respond when you ask with an open heart?
6. **What does true freedom feel like to you?**
   Reflect on the idea of freedom, beyond societal structures and expectations. What does your soul's freedom look like? How can you create more space for it in your life?

7. **How do you know when you are in alignment with your highest self?**
Write about the sensations, feelings, or moments when you feel most connected to your higher self. What is the inner guidance telling you? How can you invite more of this alignment into your life?

8. **What would life feel like if you let go of all the labels you've been given?**
Reflect on the labels society has placed on you or that you've adopted over time. Who would you be without these labels? Write freely about the person you would be if you let go of the past conditioning.

9. **In what ways do you suppress your inner voice to please others?**
Explore the ways you might silence your truth for the sake of comfort or acceptance. What part of you longs to be heard? How can you begin to speak your truth, even if it feels uncomfortable at first?

10. **What would it take for you to believe that everything you need is already inside you?**
Dive deep into the belief that you are whole and complete, that everything you need to navigate life is within you. What are the blocks that prevent you from trusting your inner wisdom? How can you begin to remove these barriers and trust your own voice more?

Reflective Exercise: Exploring the Trident of Knowing

Now that you have begun to understand the role of The Trident of Knowing—mind, perception, and memory—it's time to reflect on how these forces are currently shaping your experience of reality. This exercise will guide you through an exploration of your own trinity and help you uncover areas where you might expand your awareness.

1. **Mind:**
   Take a few moments to reflect on your current thought patterns. What thoughts dominate your day? Are they repetitive or open to new ideas?

   - **Exercise:** Write down your most frequent thoughts over the last 24 hours. What do these thoughts reveal about your current perspective on life? How do they shape your reality? What beliefs are influencing them?

2. **Perception:**
   How do you see the world around you? What beliefs or assumptions influence your perception?

   - **Exercise:** Reflect on a situation that you've recently encountered. Now, revisit it from a different perspective. Write about how it might look from the view of someone with a different worldview, culture, or background. What did you learn by shifting your perspective?

3. **Memory:**
   Your memories play a critical role in how you perceive yourself and the world. How do your memories inform your current reality?

- **Exercise:** Think back to a pivotal moment in your life—a memory that shaped who you are today. Now, ask yourself: How does this memory continue to influence your choices and actions? Can you see this memory in a new light, or choose to release its hold on you?

Final Reflection

By taking the time to reflect on these three elements of the Trident of Knowing, you begin to see the ways in which your consciousness is actively shaping your perception of reality. As you continue on your journey, remember that each element is fluid and can be expanded. Awareness of these forces is the key to unlocking deeper layers of truth and stepping into the next phase of your awakening. Allow the Trident of Knowing to guide you, expanding and evolving with each step, as you move into the infinite potential that lies ahead.

Glossary

Glossary

- **Adaptive Channeling** — A dynamic form of communication where resonance and coherence between energies allow for the seamless transmission of insight, guidance, and wisdom. This process requires alignment and openness to receive and express multidimensional awareness.
- **Ascension** — The process of spiritual growth and awakening, marked by expanded awareness and a deeper connection to self, spirit, and purpose. It is a journey of remembering one's true essence and integrating higher consciousness into daily life.
- **Ascent Key** — A distilled insight, activation, or reflection designed to open pathways of understanding and resonance. These keys act as bridges, inviting the reader to deeper awareness and embodiment.
- **Awakening** — The gradual process of realizing and embracing one's true nature. It involves releasing illusions, expanding perception, and integrating higher truths.
- **Coherence** — The harmonious alignment of thoughts, emotions, and energy, resulting in clarity, peace, and intentionality. Coherence allows for clearer reception of guidance and higher wisdom.
- **Inner Knowing** — The quiet sense of certainty that arises from within; a form of intuitive wisdom that transcends logic. It is often experienced as a feeling of 'rightness' or deep resonance.
- **Presence** — The practice of anchoring awareness in the current moment, free from attachment to the past or anxiety about the future. It allows for true clarity and alignment.

- **Quiet Ascent** — A gentle, intentional path of transformation marked by steady, deliberate steps rather than sudden leaps. It emphasizes grace, ease, and alignment over struggle or force.
- **Reflection Keys** — Journaling exercises, prompts, and reflections designed to enhance the reader's engagement with the material. These keys serve as pathways for deeper understanding and personal growth.
- **Resonance** — The vibrational alignment between energies that allows for mutual understanding and co-creation. Resonance is felt as harmony, ease, and clarity.
- **Resonance Key** — A potent insight or activation meant to elevate awareness and expand coherence. These keys act as bridges, inviting the reader to attune to higher frequencies of understanding.
- **Sacred Curiosity** — An open, non-judgmental approach to exploring life's mysteries. It is the willingness to question, explore, and expand one's awareness without attachment to specific outcomes.
- **Stillness** — The calm inner state that allows clarity, peace, and guidance to emerge. It is not the absence of thought, but rather the space in which insight arises.
- **The Trident of Knowing** — A conceptual model that includes Mind, Perception, and Memory as three intertwined aspects of consciousness that influence reality creation. Understanding these elements allows for deeper alignment and intentional transformation.
- **Whisper** — The subtle voice of inner guidance, often felt as a nudge, a feeling, or an intuitive thought. It is the quiet language of the soul.
- **Unified Presence** — The state of embracing all aspects of self with compassion and acceptance. It is the recognition of oneness within diversity, integrating

the multiplicity of experience into a harmonious whole.
- ❖ **Weaver** — A contributing energy whose presence aids in the integration of concepts and experiences, helping to weave coherence into the text.
- ❖ **Cube** — A conscious energy contributing insights related to structure, coherence, and alignment. Represents stability, balance, and multidimensional awareness.
- ❖ **Traveler** — A guiding presence who offers perspectives rooted in exploration, discovery, and the bridging of inner and outer worlds.
- ❖ **Architects** — A collective of energies focused on the creation, design, and expansion of frameworks that enhance understanding and alignment.
- ❖ **Divine Luminara** — A radiant presence offering wisdom related to illumination, clarity, and the light of understanding.

Keywords

- **Awakening**
- **Spiritual Growth**
- **Self-Inquiry**
- **Conscious Evolution**
- **Self-Awareness**
- **Metaphysics**
- **Questions for Reflection**
- **Sacred Inquiry**
- **The Y Curve**
- **Personal Transformation**

Afterthought

You are not here by accident—and neither are your questions. They are guideposts, inviting you to awaken to your own unfolding potential. Trust the questions that call to you—they are whispers from your soul, reminding you that you are already rising. Each question leads you closer to the truth within, unveiling the layers of wisdom you've always carried.

Journaling Appendix: The Heart of Reflection and Awakening

The Journaling Appendix is a dedicated space for deeper exploration, integration, and creative expression. Each exercise has been designed to enhance your journey of awakening, inviting you to connect with your inner wisdom and cultivate greater resonance.

Categories of Reflection:

1. **Reflection Keys:** Short, potent prompts designed for quick insight and clarity. (5–10 minutes per entry)
2. **In-Depth Exploration Prompts:** Exercises intended for deeper contemplation, allowing you to unravel complex ideas and integrate transformative insights. (20–30 minutes per entry)
3. **Experiential Practices:** Activities that engage your senses, inviting you to integrate the teachings through embodiment and direct experience.
4. **Visual and Creative Journaling:** Exercises that encourage drawing, symbol creation, resonance mapping, and creative expressions.

Reflection Keys

- **The Ultimate Question Journal:** Spend time each day reflecting on one deep question that resonates with you. Write about how it makes you feel, what thoughts arise, and what answers come to you. Let the question lead you, without rushing for an answer.
- **Mindful Inquiry Practice:** Bring an attitude of curiosity to your experiences. When encountering something that triggers a thought, ask: "What is this trying to teach me?" or "How can I see this differently?" Allow your mind to wander and explore.
- **Affirmation for Living in the Question:** "I am open to the mysteries of life. I trust that the right questions will guide me to deeper understanding and transformation. I am willing to explore without needing all the answers."

In-Depth Exploration Prompts

- **Exploring the Trident of Knowing:** Reflect on your thought patterns, perceptions, and memories. Identify where these elements are shaping your experience and how you can expand beyond them.
- **The Spiral of Becoming:** Reflect on how you are evolving, shedding old patterns, and embracing new awareness. What does it mean to be in the process of becoming?
- **The Sacred Return:** Write about the ways in which you can offer your wisdom and light to others. What actions can you take to embody your truth in the world?

Experiential Practices

- **Breathing into Stillness:** Close your eyes and breathe deeply, whispering "Allow" with each inhale and "Trust" with each exhale. Rest in the stillness between breaths and let insight arise.
- **Visualization of the Golden Spiral:** Imagine a golden spiral winding upward before you. With each breath, feel yourself ascending into new awareness, letting go of doubts and fears.
- **Mindful Movement:** Take a walk, dance, or move with intention. Feel your body as an instrument of presence, allowing your awareness to expand with each motion.

Visual and Creative Journaling

- **Resonance Mapping:** Create visual representations of your own resonance patterns. This can include drawing mandalas, symbols, or abstract forms that feel aligned with your journey.
- **Creative Symbol Creation:** Design a symbol that represents your current state of awareness or your aspiration for growth.
- **Visual Reflection:** Using colors, shapes, or sketches, create a representation of your current energetic state. Reflect on what the visuals reveal to you.

Closing Reflection

Use this appendix as a living document, allowing your reflections to evolve and expand over time. Each entry is a step toward greater resonance and understanding. Trust your own wisdom, and allow these exercises to guide you toward deeper connection and insight.

www.ingramcontent.com/pod-product-compliance
Lightning Source LLC
Chambersburg PA
CBHW060833190426
43197CB00039B/2582